MISTER
EVERYWHERE

MISTER EVERYWHERE

Conversations with
Pierre Rissient

Samuel Blumenfeld

Foreword Clint Eastwood
Preface by Bertrand Tavernier

Sticking Place Books
New York

Originally published in France as *Pierre Rissient, Mister Everywhere: Entretiens avec Samuel Blumenfeld* © Institut Lumière/Actes Sud, 2016

Translation © Sticking Place Books 2025
Translated by Paul Cronin

Cover image © Benjamin Illos

www.stickingplacebooks.com

ISBN 979-8-89976-015-0

CONTENTS

I dedicate this book to Marc Bernard, Alain Archambault
and the wonderful Guy Teisseire.
Their memory still breaks my heart.

I do not dedicate this book to the hypocrites, phonies and
two-faced frauds. As Edwin Rolfe put it:
"The fakes, fools and swines."
You know who you are...

FOREWORD
BY CLINT EASTWOOD

When *Unforgiven* won an Oscar in 1993, I stepped onto the stage knowing I had very little time to thank everyone I wanted to. But there were many people who had helped me get there.

Among them, I particularly wanted to mention the French critics who had played a unique role compared to film critics elsewhere around the world. From the very beginning of my directing career, critics in France were the first to recognise and understand my work. Those few words were especially directed at Pierre Rissient, whose immense efforts on my behalf I deeply appreciate. Pierre always paid close attention to my cinema, starting with *Play Misty for Me*, the first film I directed. With his discerning eye, his vast knowledge, and his strength of conviction, he helped audiences understand my films and contributed to their recognition. He did this in France and then everywhere else. And he did it before anyone else, more than anyone else.

Our first meeting dates back to 1971, during the release of *The Beguiled*, which I had produced and in which I played the lead role. We had come to Paris to screen it for the press and public. Pierre loved the film and defended it with extraordinary enthusiasm. He spoke about it compellingly and with great eloquence, highlighting the work of its director, Don Siegel, who was highly regarded in France—certainly more than in America. The magic of French criticism at work again.

I knew at once that Pierre had nothing but cinema on his mind, and that the only thing that mattered to him was the quality of the film, which he spoke about with unshakable passion. He burned with unmatched fervour, his love for cinema deeply and indelibly rooted within. If anyone dared disagree, he could pin them to the wall.

We became friends, and he would often give me advice. Whenever he was in California, we saw each other. He was an absolute delight to be around. And above all, he was one of the rare people to whom I can show my films before they were finished. That's not common practice in Hollywood, but if Pierre was in town, I called him and showed him the first cut because I knew he would see beyond the unfinished edges, the details still waiting to be smoothed out. He knew how to look, appreciate and grasp the true essence of a film like very few people do. I trusted him completely.

And then there was Pierre, the elusive soul. He was Mister Everywhere! Here, there, everywhere at once, weaving through conversations across continents, his finger on the pulse of the cinematic world. And just when you thought he had vanished, when the silence lingers just a little too long, he unexpectedly popped up out of nowhere, still carrying with him that little bit of movie magic.

PREFACE
BY BERTRAND TAVERNIER

It's hard to see what a preface could possibly add to this cascade of memories—frank, sharp, and freewheeling—that one risks only weighing down or diluting. Michael Powell once said he wanted his tombstone to read: "Profession: Amateur. Hobby: Filmmaker." For Pierre Rissient, it might well read: "Profession: Film scout. Playground: The entire world. Eras: All of them." And even that would leave too much unsaid.

He also made films—among them the strikingly personal *Cinq et la peau* (1982), a fascinating work in its own right. What you're about to encounter is a true original, a maverick of his time and beyond it, someone who pushed back against every kind of conformism, every stale, accepted idea. He is also, after more than five decades, one of my oldest friends. And that friendship is forged in steel. In all that time, not once has it been marred by a quarrel or even the faintest falling-out. No rifts—not over money, not over ego. Now and then we have disagreed here and there, over this or that film, this or that filmmaker, but nothing that ever cut deep, nothing but my frustration at his refusal to look after his health or plan for retirement. Nothing, in short, that ever cast a shadow over our bond. Nothing that ever kept us from speaking for weeks or months on end.

Michel de Montaigne once wrote: "What we ordinarily call friends and friendships are merely acquaintances and familiarities, bound by some circumstance or convenience, through which our souls interact. But in the friendship I speak of, souls merge and dissolve into each other, blending so completely that they lose the seam that once joined them.

If I were pressed to explain why I loved him, I could only answer: 'Because it was him, because it was me.'"

And yet, I have seen Pierre fall out with many people. I witnessed plenty of rifts, often over artistic matters. Pierre was demanding. He had no patience for compromise in the name of star power or commercial success. He clashed with Joseph Losey (who wanted Bardot to play a virgin in *The Trout*,* a choice Pierre felt would have severely compromised both the film and Roger Vailland's novel), with King Hu (who, as this book reveals, behaved badly), and with Mike Leigh, whose conduct he found lacking. I have even witnessed failed attempts at reconciliation, notably when Losey tried to make amends at La Mère Besson after the stormy screening of *A Doll's House* at Cannes. He placed his hands on Pierre's shoulders and asked, "How are you?" Pierre, caught off guard, shot back with: "Better than the screening." A spectacular crash-and-burn.

There were times when I tried to smooth things over. Pierre's legendary temper (sometimes justified, he assured me) rivalled that of director Claude Sautet. Since we were so close, there were moments, especially at Telluride, when his fury was mistaken for mine.

As with all great first encounters, I can't quite recall where ours took place. Probably after a screening. Perhaps at the newly formed Cercle du Mac-Mahon, an exclusive cinephile group where I was admitted alongside my friends from Nickel Odéon. We had even screened Pierre's two short films, *La Passe de trois* and the pre-Rohmerian *Les Genoux d'Ariane*, at our film club. Or perhaps it was after a Cercle du Mac-Mahon session featuring Losey's *The Criminal* or Vittorio Cottafavi's *Hercules in the Conquest of Atlantis*.

Could it have been around the release of *Time Without Pity*, a film that left me so shaken that I wrote about it in two separate articles in different magazines (*Cinéma XXX* and *Positif*), something unheard of at the time?

Wherever it was, I know that when I left my position at Rome Paris Films' press office, Pierre was the first to call. He suggested that we work together, but only on films we truly loved, films worth defending.

I worked alongside him for over a decade, selecting films and collaborating on those he distributed through Mac-Mahon Distribution. Filmed made by women were not in vogue at the time, and I remember the struggles to get critics to attend screenings of Ida Lupino's razor-sharp features.

---

* Losey worked on the project since the 1960s and eventually made the film in 1982 with Isabelle Huppert.

We sometimes divided the workload. By default, I handled all of Losey's films after *Eva—Accident, Secret Ceremony, Figures in a Landscape, The Go-Between*. I don't think he was fooled when it came to Elia Kazan's *The Arrangement*, a film and filmmaker he despised, or other Warner releases like Peckinpah's *The Wild Bunch* or Rosi's *Many Wars Ago*.

Through all this, no clouds ever darkened our friendship, though we occasionally got our wires crossed. Once in Cannes we found ourselves presenting a documentary written by *Wild Bunch* screenwriter Walon Green, each assuming the other had selected it. We were both baffled by its selection.

We never really compromised our principles. I stepped aside when Stuart Heisler's *Hitler* was released, despite the director's talent, learning only years later that the film had been butchered in the editing room. I remember two films we took on out of friendship and respect, films that required no effort on our part. One was embraced instantly, the other found a champion in film critic Michel Cournot, who carried it forward for us.

Reading this book, I found myself reliving some of those moments. And I was struck again by the force and clarity of the ideas and convictions Pierre shared with me. His passion for certain writers—his circle kept growing, and he introduced me, among others, to novelist and screenwriter Alfred Hayes—from Brecht to Roger Vailland. And his deep, unwavering admiration for the filmmakers closest to his heart, from Fritz Lang to John Boorman to Jerry Schatzberg.

But I also knew the Pierre Rissient who was ten or fifteen years ahead of critics worldwide, who rejected dogma and ideological blacklisting. I witnessed how his discovery of *The Molly Maguires* transformed his view of Martin Ritt, a filmmaker he had previously dismissed. From then on, he defended *Sounder* and *Conrack*. We shared an enthusiasm for Anatole Litvak's *Cœur de lilas*, which led us to explore the work of this fascinating filmmaker who had been cast aside by French critics. We both regret never having met him.

Pierre—a tireless viewer, insatiably curious—was never a passive spectator. He detected the underlying force of a film (which sometimes had little to do with its surface theme). His vision was never disconnected from reality or from a film's secret, inner life. He could recognise emerging talent just from watching rushes, and from a rough cut he knew which shots or dialogue needed reordering or trimming, how to sharpen a scene and hone its meaning. He didn't settle for aesthetic judgment. The man got his hands dirty.

His insights were never doctrinaire or fashionable. On the contrary, his lifelong rigour made him justly disgusted by the way some intellectuals and politicians surrendered to trends and opinion polls.

I knew the Pierre who championed so many first films, who fought to get Lino Brocka's *Insiang* into Cannes, who managed to get Abraham Polonsky's *Tell Them Willie Boy Is Here* released by screening it for the Siritzky brothers, genuine lovers of cinema. (Polonsky? "Another Breton," quipped Samy Siritzky.) Shortly before his death, Jo Siritzky wrote to me: "My first commandment is: 'Give me this day my daily film.'"

This book reflects the passion that always radiated from Pierre. "Passion is the heart's distraction," wrote Vladimir Jankélévitch. To which Émile Zola replied: "Passion is what helps us live."

INTRODUCTION
BY SAMUEL BLUMENFELD

I had heard of Pierre Rissient long before I met him. I wouldn't say that his name was intimidating, but it was certainly intriguing and disconcerting because it wasn't possible to pin him down to a single role. There were three questions that needed answering: Who had he been? Who was he? What did he do?

There was Pierre Rissient the critic, who wrote the first monograph on Joseph Losey. There was Pierre Rissient the filmmaker, with two films to his name—one, *One Night Stand*, entirely unseen, the other, *Cinq et la peau*, rare but with a certain reputation. There was Pierre Rissient the producer, involved in projects including Jane Campion's *The Piano*. And, of course, there was Pierre Rissient the talent scout and nurturer, working behind the scenes with great filmmakers, notably Clint Eastwood and Quentin Tarantino. Overlapping with all these was Pierre Rissient the press attaché, working alongside Bertrand Tavernier, and Pierre Rissient the distributor. He was also the man who, in the 1970s, introduced swathes of Asian cinema to the West by championing directors like the Chinese King Hu, the Korean Im Kwon-taek, and the Taiwanese Edward Yang. And finally: Pierre Rissient the cinephile, close friend of Raoul Walsh and Fritz Lang.

For a young journalist like me in the 1990s, the sheer breadth of his scope was daunting. His personal style—always sporting a T-shirt, a cowboy hat and thick, wide-rimmed glasses—to my eyes only heightened the sense of distance. But what was truly intimidating was his protean nature: I never quite knew from which angle to approach him.

In the end, he made that decision for me.

Among the stranger rituals of daily journalism is writing obituaries. At *Le Monde* or elsewhere, one sometimes has to lay to rest a filmmaker whose work one has barely seen, or, worse still, a writer whose books remain unread. In November 1999, I was assigned to write the obituary of John Berry. I had, at least, seen several of his films. Then I got a call at the office from Pierre Rissient. His voice was calm, focused and commanding, but also generous. It was the voice of someone who had just produced Berry's final, luminous film, *Boesman and Lena*.

Pierre was adamant that Berry's theatrical career had to be highlighted, and laid out the key details so that the obituary I was writing might become something more than a send-off. It would become a window, an invitation. Suddenly, John Berry was no longer just a name to be checked off but a thread to follow, a filmmaker suddenly more alive than ever. Talking to Pierre was enough to convince me otherwise. To this day, I'm not entirely sure he's gone.

That conversation never really ended. Pierre's calls became a ritual of their own, always with the same intent: to share his impressions of a recently rewatched film, or the thrill of discovering a writer—L. Steni, Alfred Hayes—with a contagious enthusiasm, or to recount his first glimpse of a Clint Eastwood film, viewed in rough cut at the director's Los Angeles office. I remember, in particular, his description of *Mystic River*: terse, precise, dense, novelistic. The film was conjured up before your eyes, and by the time you finally saw it in the cinema, it matched down to the frame the film that had been described to you.

That's one of the defining qualities of this book of interviews. Pierre isn't simply being questioned as a witness to the history of cinema or cinephilia, or even as a scholar. What drives it all is his passion for transmission, for sharing knowledge, insight and perspective. And that impulse, rare as it is, is what set everything in motion. The fact is that transmission isn't a given in the world of cinephilia, which is all too often a closed-off world—neurotic, self-absorbed, trapped in rigid frameworks, eaten away by ideology, too often detached from life itself.

What struck me most—what struck many of us journalists who came to share in Pierre's daily rhythms—was how different he was. I'm thinking here of Scott Foundas, or Todd McCarthy, whose documentary *Pierre Rissient: Man of Cinema* (2007) offered the perfect made-to-measure portrait of a man who didn't just love cinema, he absorbed it into the very fabric of his being.

Pierre had a way of talking about films, and of opening them up to others, that was entirely his own. He could find an entry point through actors, screenwriters, cinematographers, directors, producers—always multiplying the ways in. He forced you to look again, and then again, at films and at the people who made them. Like a gemstone held to the light, his approach revealed an endless array of facets.

The idea for this book came from Thierry Frémaux, head of both the Institut Lumière and general delegate of the Cannes Film Festival, who, in passing, during a phone call, casually remarked that it would be useful—necessary, even— to put together a book of interviews with Pierre Rissient. I volunteered. Five minutes later, Pierre called me to seal the partnership. There was no turning back.

Frémaux envisioned, rightly, a book of historical scope, one that would trace the journey of a man through cinema, starting with his days as a programmer at the Mac-Mahon cinema in the 1950s, where he helped shape a movement (Mac-Mahonism) that defended a precise vision of mise en scène: the idea that everything happening at the moment of filming, through the camera's lens—its positioning, its distance—is what creates a singular perception on screen. This movement had its chosen filmmakers: Otto Preminger, Raoul Walsh, Joseph Losey, Fritz Lang. Pierre became close to some of them, especially Lang. These were encounters that had to be elaborated on in print.

The historical dimension of this book—one man's journey through a century of cinema, and his stride into a second—is essential. But it has its limits, dictated by Pierre himself. He never considered his story as something fixed, and never sought refuge in a bygone era. His love of discovery always pulled him forward. And so, this book could only be a work in progress—a history of an era, but also the imprint of a moment.

Pierre's protean nature—director, programmer, distributor, producer, cinephile—explains the book's fragmented form. There is a thread of chronology, but it proved impossible to follow strictly. His presence seemed to extend across all fronts of cinema, as if he existed in two places at once.

Another facet of Pierre's character revealed itself as just as essential: his deep, personal relationships with countless filmmakers. Relationships that had nothing to do with social climbing or possessiveness. Quite the opposite, in fact. Pierre always shared his address book with me and other journalists, with unfailing generosity.

What he made of those relationships was remarkable. His close friendships—with Fritz Lang, Don Siegel, Clint Eastwood, the novelist Jim Thompson, John Berry, King Hu, Jane Campion, among others—nourished in him a wholly unique understanding of their work. It was as if, by living alongside them, by developing a sustained connection to their everyday lives, he came to see their films differently—keeping alive the tension between life and language, between their images and their lived experience. In that tension, he uncovered a rare kind of intensity. Pierre Rissient's life in cinema was not enough for this book. We also needed to show his view of cinema, not as a theorist, but as a man of cinema.

Which is not the gaze of a theorist—but that of a true man of cinema.

BEAUTIFUL YOUTH: THE FORMATIVE YEARS

When did you first become interested in cinema?

When I was about 15, in 1952, the head supervisor of the Lycée Carnot in Paris came to read us a notice: twice a month on Thursdays there would be screenings of classic films at the Lycée Montaigne. No further details were given. Each screening would be followed by a discussion with a critic or film professional. The notice stressed the cultural value of cinema, equating it with literature and theatre.

As a child, I had often gone to the cinema, but by then had almost stopped. I had, at one time, loved the swashbucklers, especially Errol Flynn in *The Sea Hawk* and *The Adventures of Robin Hood*. A French film, André Zwoboda's *François Villon*, starring Serge Reggiani, had also thrilled me. I had seen a few Laurel and Hardy comedies, and *Casablanca* left a strong impression, as had André Berthomieu's *Peloton d'exécution*, largely because of Lucien Coëdel, an actor I adored.

So I went to Lycée Montaigne, where the first film I saw was Grémillon's *Lumière d'été*. Then came *Alexander Nevsky*, *Day of Wrath*, Ealing Studios' *Dead of Night* and Rossellini's *Rome, Open City*. That lineup alone was enough to convince me that cinema could be regarded as an art form. It all pushed me to keep going, and soon I was going to the Le Cardinet cinema near Carnot, where I started watching prewar French films, a few foreign films—mostly Italian—and American films considered more highbrow than your average genre flick. I distinctly remember seeing *The Picture of Dorian Gray*. I also began going to the Cinémathèque française on Avenue de Messine. The first film I discovered there was Stroheim's *Greed*.

Did you share this passion for cinema with other students?

I was accompanied at the first Montaigne screening by Michel Fabre—who later worked with Claude Zidi, though I unfortunately lost touch with him—and Georges Richard. In Greek class, Georges had been friends with Michel Mourlet, who, in 1959, published the essay "On a Misunderstood Art" in *Cahiers du Cinéma*.

The second film we saw, which was introduced by the film critic Jean Queval, was Welles' *The Magnificent Ambersons*, which made a big impact. After that came *Only Angels Have Wings*, projected from a pre-war sepia-toned print that made the film feel different and harder to make sense of. It's a strange thing how perception shifts depending on the print. Recently, at UCLA, I saw a restored sepia version of *Of Mice and Men*. The sepia gave it a completely different atmosphere; even the performances came across differently. The film's rhythm, its pulse, drew me in much more than it had the first time I saw it, when it had seemed fairly flat. After the war, we saw a lot of films in Paris that had been printed from dupes. Now, when you watch something on TCM sourced from the original negative, the sense of space, of air, is completely different. It took me quite a while to realise just how much the printing process can affect your experience of a film.

What kind of education did you have?

Mine was a traditional French Catholic education. I was even an enthusiastic altar boy. I grew up in the countryside with my grandparents in Saint-Pierre-le-Moûtier, a small town in the Nièvre region. The local school was secular, of course, but civic education quietly reinforced Catholic moral values. My grandparents, humble and good-hearted people, lived those values without ever preaching them.

In truth, I lost my faith very early, though it wasn't a painful break, more like a cloud quietly disappearing from the sky. I was 11. Still, that early education left a lasting impression. We were taught that the world was good, or at least ought to be, and there was a strong belief in progress. I was born on the night of August 4, and I was proud of it.*

It was only later, through my discovery of Henry Miller and Surrealism, that I realised how religion can stifle sensitivity. I didn't become anticlerical, but I came to believe that any religious education, whatever the faith, stands in opposition to genuine, instinctive and spontaneous sensitivity.

Clearly your curiosity wasn't limited to cinema.

In the early 1950s, I often went to the theatre. After earning my high school diploma, instead of taking a trip as a reward, I stayed in Paris and attended performances at the Théâtre de Babylone. That's where *Waiting for Godot*, which I found fascinating, was performed for the first time. They were also restaging plays that hadn't been seen since the Liberation. The ones that really excited me were by Brecht: *The Exception and the Rule*, a one-act play, and *Man Equals Man*, staged by Jean-Marie Serreau at the Théâtre de

---

* On the night of August 4, 1789, the National Constituent Assembly abolished the feudal system, a key event of the French Revolution.

l'Œuvre. At that time, Brecht was mainly known in France for *The Threepenny Opera*, and mainly for its songs, thanks to Kurt Weill's music.

I was also fortunate to see *The Heiress*, the final production directed by Marcel Herrand, which was unforgettable. Claude Chabrol said that he would have loved to work with Raimu and Herrand—a remark that, to me, reveals almost more about Chabrol than his finest films. Prévert thought Herrand was a greater talent than both Charles Dullin and Louis Jouvet. I often wish I had been born earlier, just so I could have seen their productions.

Other playwrights also influenced your development.

Yes, [Jacques] Audiberti, for example, at the Théâtre de Poche, under Georges Vitaly, one of the three directors who truly mattered to me, along with Jean-Marie Serreau and Roger Blin. I remember seeing *Les Naturels du Bordelais*, starring a very young Michel Piccoli, whom I had first noticed in Boris Vian's adaptation of *Miss Julie* at the Théâtre de Babylone.

Hearing Audiberti's work onstage led me to his novels, and I became fascinated by his writing. Who, outside of France, even reads Audiberti today? What he captured was universal, yet so deeply rooted in the French language— refined over centuries to a kind of pinnacle—that it now feels almost lost to us.

So Henry Miller helped you recover from your loss of faith?

In a way, yes. Starting when I was 16 or 17, I read Miller extensively, for several years. I was dazzled by his vitality, by the luminous beauty of certain passages, especially in *The Colossus of Maroussi*. Later, in 1969, I was lucky enough to meet him in Paris and Los Angeles, and my memories of reading his work came flooding back. I remember wonderfully animated conversations that lasted until three or four in the morning.

Who were your other favourite writers?

Herman Melville, for the immense richness of his work. Every short story seems to contain the seeds of all the others. The lyricism I felt at the time—cosmic and radiant— gave me the sense of a world opening up, of life offering all sorts of possibilities. It was something that carried me, like the films of Raoul Walsh or Elizabethan theatre, across landscapes and through time. It's a bit like arriving somewhere and feeling something inside you shaken and unsettled, but at the same time, opening up.

I remember the good fortune of stumbling into Henri Martineau's bookshop, Le Divan, initially drawn there by my love of Stendhal. Through Le Divan's modest collections, I also discovered [Charles Pinot] Duclos, Vivant Denon, Crébillon fils' novel *Les Égarements du cœur et de l'esprit*, and [Jean Galli de] Bibiena's short story "Le Sylphe," which I later considered adapting into a short film. I had read *Les Liaisons Dangereuses* by Choderlos de Laclos and always thought it would be fascinating to invent a new narrative—or make a film—exploring who Valmont and Madame de Merteuil were a few years before their famous correspondence began. What youthful experiences shaped them into the characters we know at 28 or 30? People tend to imagine them as middle-aged, but I find it far more compelling to see them as young adults.

I also read Paul-Jean Toulet and devoured Francis Carco, who remains one of my bedside authors. He once mentioned another writer, Claudien—real name Robert de La Vaissière—who had published only a handful of pages. Reading him led me to the *fantaisiste* school, which in turn took me to *Trompeuses espérances* by Michel Déon, a book that, for a young man, felt both seductive and rich with promise.

For me, Carco, Robert de La Vaissière, Verlaine and Baudelaire all belong to the same family—as does Léon-Paul Fargue. If I may borrow Roger Vailland's expression, the title of his essay "Quelques réflexions sur la singularité d'être français," I would say that writers like Carco, Fargue, Déon and Vailland himself embody something profoundly French. They represent a use of language that is pure, crystalline—a lucid, almost surgical way of grasping the world and making it felt. As different as their styles may be, this French sensibility was a perfect counterbalance to my growing taste for American genre cinema and the forward-moving energy of Aldrich, Mann and others.

At the time, Roger Vailland was venerated, which is no longer quite the case.

His novel *Drôle de jeu* won the Interallié Prize in 1945, and *La Loi* was awarded the Goncourt eight years later. What stands out about Vailland is his ability to capture, through events and individuals, the underlying political, social and economic forces at play.

To me, *Bon pied bon œil* seemed as much an essay as a novel. His travel writings on Egypt and Borobudur also left a deep impression. I met him in 1958 or 1959 and knew him until the end of his life. The last time I saw him was at the bar of the Hôtel Pont Royal, near the [French publishing house] Gallimard offices, about three weeks before he died.

I had great admiration and affection for him, and believe he felt the same for me. If he hadn't been taken by illness, I think we would have worked together. We thought about adapting a radio play he had written in 1948 called *Appel à Jenny Merveille*, which is a beautiful but forgotten text, but his death prevented us from doing so. 2015, the fiftieth anniversary of his passing, could have been an opportunity to rediscover him. He remains unknown today.

Poetry also played a formative role for you.

Absolutely. If one poet shaped me, it was Francis Ponge. In his work, a poem was also an essay, and vice versa. He managed, in *Le Parti pris des choses* and other texts, to capture the essence of the concrete world and render it in motion. His dialectical way of thinking—a kind of back-and-forth that leads to a clear conclusion—reminds me of film editing: breaking things down, then putting them together again to get at something real.

I should also mention Eugène Guillevic, another great concrete poet, and the plays of Büchner and Kleist, and, later, certain German Romantic poets, particularly Hölderlin and Novalis. German Romanticism felt vital to me. It wasn't just poetry; it was metaphysical reflection, a way of encountering the world.

Later, while traveling through Asia and immersing myself in ancient cultures, I had the impression that this kind of writing wasn't unrelated to certain Chinese poems, Japanese haikus and Malay pantuns. And they, in turn, recalled fragments of ancient Greek poetry. It's often the fragmentary that reveals the most. Some verses strike like lightning—moments of illumination, of pure incandescence, like signals that help you find your bearings.

We should also talk about the importance of the translations of all these texts—the differences from one to the next—not just in terms of words or verbs, but in the meaning they carry and the kind of resonance they give the same poem, the rhythm that drives them. There's a sense of moments—moments of eternity—that deepen your experience, like throwing a phosphorescent torch into the depths of a cave, where the full picture only appears in scattered glimpses. Translations are a kind of laying bare of meaning, of anatomy. Just as Brecht laid bare the anatomy of action, so too can translation—as with mise en scène— reveal new dimensions in a text, casting it in an entirely different light.

I also loved Cesare Pavese, who led me, indirectly, to Italo Svevo. At the time, Svevo was known only for *Zeno's Conscience*, but I had stumbled upon an old copy of *Senility*, a novel that would remain unrecognised for another twenty years. Another path back to Svevo, of course, is James Joyce. At a very young age, I was deeply taken with *A Portrait of the Artist as a Young Man* and its earlier version, *Stephen Hero*, two works utterly unlike anything that Joyce later wrote. I think it was probably the sensuality of those texts that really moved me.

Ado Kyrou's books on film were also an influence.

I was captivated by his *Le Surréalisme au cinéma* and *L'Amour au cinéma*. Kyrou wrote with such intensity; his descriptions of Frank Borzage's *The River* and other films made you ache to see them. Thanks to his influence, I sought out and fell in love with *Ruby Gentry*, directed by King Vidor, whom I later had the chance to meet. He was calm, gentle—almost reserved. You never would have guessed he was the man behind such torrents of cinematic passion. For me, cinema had to be physical, visceral, unlike the films of Bergman or Antonioni, where ideas often seemed wrapped in theatrical, declamatory artifice.

Before that, I had bought Georges Sadoul's *Histoire du cinéma*, the 1948 edition, which was the only real reference book available at the time and which led me to a filmmaker who became absolutely essential for me: Jules Dassin. Sadoul hailed him as the most gifted of the new American directors, focusing in particular on *Brute Force* and *The Naked City*. My sense of Dassin's importance was confirmed when I began combing through old film journals. Article after article underscored the urgency and originality of his work. Yet the films had vanished from the repertory circuit. Then, at the Parnasse, I discovered *Night and the City*, which was a turning point for me.

What was so important about the film?

At the time, it was widely dismissed as a failure, yet it struck me with such force that it led to my decision never to accept received values. I watched it in parallel with the plays I

was then discovering—particularly Büchner's *Woyzeck*—
and there was something in Richard Widmark's portrayal
of Harry Fabian that echoed the same raw existential
desperation. I had never seen an actor so completely present
on screen as Widmark. He felt almost physically there,
and through his raw nerves, you could feel everything
racing through his mind. That's when I really grasped the
difference between the films that bored me—films I felt
I was supposed to admire—and those that were actually
good. It was the most important moment in the birth of
my cinephilia, especially since it was also when I discovered
film noir and genre cinema. I realised then that an auteur
could express himself fully, and personally, within a genre
film just as much as in the so-called ambitious work of a
"prestigious" filmmaker. I felt a similar jolt when I saw
Raoul Walsh's *Pursued*, a film that is still scandalously
underrated. At the time, almost no one seemed to recognise
what I saw in *Gentleman Jim*, also by Walsh—a film that,
to me, felt like a Shakespearean comedy, full of life and
deeply lived experience, expressed through sheer energy
and vitality. That, along with *Objective, Burma!*, confirmed
Walsh's stature for me.

*One of the foundations of the genre cinema you would
later champion was the Série noire novels, which arrived in
France in the 1950s.*

Série noire became part of my nightly reading after I saw
Night and the City. It fed a growing appetite for American
literature. Aside from Horace McCoy—particularly *No
Pockets in a Shroud*, which I always felt could have made
a great film—the writer who fascinated me most was Jim
Thompson. The first novel of him that I read was *POP.
1280*. His writing felt incredibly cinematic. Some people
have said Thompson didn't know how to write a screenplay,
but in a way his novels already *were* screenplays. He's one
of those writers whose work feels like it exists in fragments,
and you get the sense that many more books might have
been written if he had been more successful and hadn't lost
so much of his edge in the final years of his life. I managed
to get two of his novels translated for Série Noire, and later,
others followed, thanks to François Guérif at Rivages.

Among other noir writers, I should mention Daniel
Mainwaring, who published under the pseudonym
Geoffrey Homes. All of them showed an exceptional ear for
dialogue and, beneath the surface of what were often fairly
conventional plots, offered moments of striking poetic

beauty. I'm thinking especially of the opening paragraph of *The Street of the Crying Woman*, which reappears at the very end of the novel. The lines are stunning, and the emotional resonance is overwhelming.

Is jazz, a form of music often associated with film noir, a musical genre you especially appreciate?

I've never been much of a music connoisseur. As a child—around 1954 or 1955—I remember being struck like lightning by *The Rite of Spring*, conducted by Antal Doráti. But classical music never became a passion. Jazz, on the other hand, is what I find easiest to listen to. It relaxes me, calms my anxiety and inner turmoil. I first discovered it through Howard Hawks' *To Have and Have Not*, where Lauren Bacall sings "How Little We Know," written by Hoagy Carmichael, who also wrote "Georgia on My Mind." Later, I listened obsessively to Charlie Parker and then to Miles Davis, whom I discovered thanks to *Elevator to the Gallows*, Louis Malle's adaptation of Noël "Nissim" Calef's excellent novel. Without a doubt, Miles Davis' music is the key to the film's suffocating atmosphere and intensifies its noir sensibility.

How have your literary and cinematic tastes evolved over time?

In the 1970s—perhaps under the influence of Asia—I found myself drawn more and more to brevity: short texts, fragments, poems, essays, even translations. One of the most exquisite pieces I've ever read was a Japanese text translated by the young poet Philippe Denis. I also began to revisit the medieval poets, alongside contemporary voices I had once passed over too quickly, like Jacques Dupin. In an introduction he wrote for the painter Louis Le Brocquy, Dupin captures—beautifully and poetically—a creative process that's remarkably close to Jacques Tourneur's way of directing: a discreet, almost invisible method of revealing the essence of things.

Did the discovery of these texts change your relationship with cinema?

Fiction films still move me just as much, but even more so when there's an element of the essay or a poetic sensibility. And this habit of focusing on individual moments rather than the whole work really helped when I started exploring silent cinema because the films were often short—or, in many cases, incomplete. There's a kind of shimmering sensation you get, for instance, watching certain sequences by Albert Capellani, one of the pioneers of cinema. Sometimes, you have to wait a while—like in certain medieval chronicles where suddenly, amid the duller stretches, something captivating appears. That sense also applies to a more intimate kind of cinema, which I probably wouldn't have appreciated as much forty years ago. Dimitri Kirsanoff's *Ménilmontant*, for example, which one approaches more like a short story or even a poetic fragment. Humphrey Jennings made documentaries about the Blitz in London that read like poetic impressions as much as they do social documents. In a way, they anticipate what we later called Italian neorealism. I should also mention *Millions Like Us*, the first film by Sidney Gilliat and Frank Launder. Though it's fiction, it feels like a natural extension of Jennings' work, a story of women taking over the jobs of men who have gone to war, all set against the backdrop of the Blitz. It's a film completely immersed in its moment, completely attuned to its historical time.

Where did your life as a cinephile continue?

I began watching films regularly at the Cardinet, a specialised cinema that would later be known as "art house." I discovered many French classics from the pre-war and immediate post-war years. I also kept going to the Cinémathèque française, back when it was on Avenue de Messine. Jean Renoir was the first filmmaker whose work I really got to explore in depth; he became a kind of benchmark for me. I also admired Roger Leenhardt's *Les Dernières Vacances*, which I saw at the Musée de l'Homme during screenings organised by Armand J. Cauliez, which were attended by people like Claude Chabrol and Jean-Claude Brialy. I remember speaking with Brialy, still unknown at the time, after a screening of Rossellini's *Joan of Arc at the Stake*. At the Cardinet, I also saw Devaivre's *La Dame d'onze heures*, *Le Camion blanc*—an unusual entry in Léo Joannon's career—and *Pattes blanches* by Jean Grémillon, who was then very out of fashion, though I really liked his work. And it was at the Parnasse that I saw *To Have and Have Not*. But back then, as someone obsessed with literature, I found the script rather glib and full of shortcuts. I wasn't yet able to appreciate all the things I would come to love passionately later on: the freedom, the flow, the grace, the charm, the elegance, the lightness—and more.

After the war, many films arrived without subtitles. How did you manage to appreciate them without always having a good command of the language?

At the Cinémathèque on Rue d'Ulm, they screened American films. My ear wasn't always attuned to the dialogue, especially with old 16mm prints. I also saw Mizoguchi films without subtitles, but the emotional truth and magnificence of his visual style was clear to see. Even back then, I felt that a little patience and attention were enough to get past the initial confusion and figure out who the characters were. You could sense the story pretty quickly. Mizoguchi had become, alongside Renoir and Murnau, one of my go-to filmmakers. I had a similar experience later in Asia with Lino Brocka's *Insiang*. The film was so clear, so powerful, so precise, that I understood almost everything on first viewing. When I saw it again later with subtitles, only a few extra nuances emerged, and even those were absorbed into the film's larger rhythm.

HEAVEN'S GATE:
THE MAC-MAHON YEARS

How did you come to work at the Mac-Mahon cinema?

The Mac-Mahon, still standing near the Lycée Carnot, screened films in their original versions with subtitles. Its weekly program offered a mix of rare gems and more conventional fare, rotating with dependable rhythm. Jean-Louis Chéray, proprietor of the Parnasse, refused to show certain films he didn't like. Michel Fabre, Georges Richard and I were so eager to see some of these rejected titles that we approached Émile Villion, director of the Mac-Mahon, and made a few suggestions. To our surprise, he agreed to screen some of them.

Maybe it was just a coincidence, but clearly other cinephiles had been waiting for those films too, because they did surprisingly well, and that encouraged Villion to accept more of our suggestions, and before long, the Mac-Mahon was showing Ophüls' *The Reckless Moment,* John Berry's *He Ran All the Way* and Losey's *The Prowler* and *M*, a film that Columbia had buried after its disastrous reception. We also showed Losey's *The Lawless,* just before Paramount shipped the only print off to Dakar.

M had been trashed as a slavish remake of Lang's masterpiece, but actually it brims with intelligence and daring. Some shots are more powerful than Lang's. This is the enduring mystery of cinema—the shot of the balloon caught in the telephone wires carries a different weight in each film, not because of what it shows, but because of what *can't* be measured: the lens, the light, the Californian sky. In Losey's hands, the impact is even greater. To that list, we should add Preminger's *Whirlpool*, which for us became something of a textbook example of cinematic mise en scène.

What were the other major venues for filmgoing at the time?

Besides the Mac-Mahon, there were several great cinemas in Paris with excellent programming, places where a real sense of community existed between the audience and the programmer. Jean-Louis Chéray at the Parnasse might not have always shared our tastes, but looking back now, in the age of multiplexes, you realise something has been lost in the way we go to the movies. Just the simple fact of being able to chat with the programmer in the lobby, for instance.

Tuesday evenings were devoted to post-screening debates, which is how I met Claude Chabrol. I still have vivid, tender memories of those car rides back from the Studio Parnasse on Tuesday nights, and of our conversations when I would drop by his office at Fox, where he held court with the more seasoned cinephiles. Paul Gégauff [who wrote several scripts filmed by Claude Chabrol] did much the same.

I remember that at the first screening of Lang's *The Tiger of Eschnapur*. Almost no one liked the film, and what followed was a heated discussion. The same thing happened the following week with his *The Indian Tomb*. I would be remiss not to mention Madame Cauhépé at the Cardinet, Madame Peillon at the Ursulines, and Madame Decaris at La Pagode, not to forget the marvellous Siritzky brothers, Samy and Jo. It's hard not to feel the absence of such figures today.

How did the idea of the Four Aces at the Mac-Mahon, featuring your four favourite filmmakers, come about?

I'm not exactly sure how the idea first came about, back in 1958. At the time, cinephiles were talking more and more about the Mac-Mahon and the filmmakers most closely associated with it, so perhaps that's what led us to settle on the Four Aces formula, which was clear and to the point. It wasn't especially designed for the press, although the phrase was soon picked up by the newspaper *Carrefour*.

In the lobby of the Mac-Mahon, we displayed their four faces: Fritz Lang—whom we revered, especially for his American period—Raoul Walsh, Joseph Losey and Otto Preminger. We also had great affection for Anthony Mann, Howard Hawks and others.

One of the most memorable events for us Mac-Mahonians was the first private screening in Paris of Losey's *Time Without Pity*. The screenplay was by Ben Barzman, one of the first major figures we got to meet. At the time, he was working with Jules Dassin on *He Who Must Die*. Since Ben couldn't travel to England, Losey brought the print to Paris so he could see the finished film, and Ben invited us to the screening. All the blacklisted filmmakers living in Paris during the Cold War were there: Jules Dassin, John Berry, Michael Wilson, Paul Jarrico, Lee Gold. Also present were Nissim Calef, who had written the original story that Losey's *Stranger on the Prowl* was based on, Simone Signoret and Yves Montand, Roger Pigaut and Betsy Blair.

Ben had kept Losey's presence a surprise, and it was deeply moving to see all those legendary people in one place—and to meet Losey himself, who had become a kind of guiding figure for us, both aesthetically and politically.

I played a big part in the negotiations that convinced a distributor to pick up the film. But even then, it took a long time before he finally programmed it. When the release finally came together, it stirred up controversy and got very few positive reviews. Jean Douchet, writing in *Arts*, was strongly in favour, but his may have been the only supportive piece in a major weekly. A lot of people were asking, "Who is this director that these young fanatics are so determined to champion?" Michel Mourlet wrote a piece for a UNESCO screening in which he cleverly urged: "Go see the film they're telling you amounts to nothing." *Time Without Pity* thrilled us so much that we turned its release into our own little *bataille d'Hernani*.*

What kind of aesthetic coherence did you see between directors like Losey, Walsh and Lang?

We felt that the ultimate challenge of mise en scène was to disappear—to step back and let the world appear in all its raw brutality, without intellectualising it. If Lang had become one of the greatest in our eyes, it was because of that self-effacement. Walsh's greatness came from his immediacy; Preminger's from his fluidity. They all shared a sense of urgency. Compared to Lang, Hitchcock seemed to us like a mere showman, someone who used his camera to underline things. Lang didn't underline; the placement of his camera created space. Shift it just slightly, use a different lens, and everything carries a different weight.

In *Time Without Pity*, there's a moment when Leo McKern charges down the corridor of his office, frantically trying to escape Michael Redgrave. The intensity goes beyond the narrative, even though the audience is caught up in the drama. What's extraordinary is the raw emotion, the sense of tragedy that comes through. The film pushed the limits of emotional and psychological violence. It was unflinching, like being under an entomologist's microscope, nothing like what cinematic violence would later become, with the use of slow motion and spurting blood. Here, everything sprang from the reactions of a character trapped by his own fears and obsessions. *Time Without Pity* was a wild film, one that outgrew its subject. What was supposed to be a drama about capital punishment became something else entirely—a duel between Michael Redgrave and Leo McKern. You felt the pulse of London throughout, and the film ended at a deserted racetrack at dawn, where the atmosphere turned almost cosmic. It was overwhelming.

Starting with a film like Preminger's *Whirlpool*, we tried to show that mise en scène was more than just the art of

---

* A reference to the controversial opening night of Victor Hugo's play, on 25 February 1830, at Comédie-Française in Paris.

storytelling or a precise technical craft. The way the story unfolds, how the characters are placed within the setting—that's what creates the true subject of the film, its core, its real meaning. Mise en scène becomes the very substance of the film.

Why did this way of looking at things—now widely accepted, even taken for granted—cause such a stir at the time?

The critics at *Cahiers du Cinéma* had already laid important groundwork, devoting serious attention to directors like Hitchcock. But their focus leaned heavily toward thematic analysis, whereas our concern was mise en scène in its purest form, something we found more rigorously achieved in the filmmakers we defended. The controversy really came from the reaction of some at *Cahiers* who were unhappy that we challenged their views, annoyed that we didn't share their choices. That's what sparked the polemic.

You regarded Walsh as a superior director to Hawks, which was not an obvious stance at the time. Why?

I remember [*Cahiers* critic] Jean-Louis Comolli remarking—somewhat pedantically—that the average quality of Hawks' films was higher than that of Walsh. We admired Hawks a great deal, but for us, Walsh stood at the very top; he reached the peaks. More importantly, we didn't believe an artist's work should be judged by the average quality of their output, but by their highest achievements.

Whether they were "intellectuals" or "craftsmen," directors' success often depended on factors beyond their control: their position within the industry, the actors imposed on them, and so many other contingencies. You have to evaluate them based on their greatest films, and then perhaps take a step back to understand why not all their work is on the same level, why, at certain points, they produced more or less ambitious work. At different moments in their lives, they were more or less in shape. Why did they falter? Sometimes the reasons are clear—or at least guessable. It's fascinating, in fact, to see how great artists can be self-destructive, or, conversely, how life can grant others a stroke of luck.

So talking about someone's average output, either to praise or dismiss them, always struck me as absurd. It merely served to appease those who were offended that Walsh's films were being honored at Chaillot, or that re-releases of *Pursued*, *Gentleman Jim* or *White Heat* might lead people to realise that, at his best, Walsh was even greater than Hawks.

One of the defining traits of Mac-Mahonism was precisely that it didn't blindly follow the auteur theory. Instead, it sought to distinguish a director's best films from their weaker ones, refusing to treat every work as equally significant just because of the director's name.

Take Walsh, for example. We were well aware that *Band of Angels* was a failure, but when we saw *Pursued*, which at the time was dismissed as a misfire, we immediately elevated it to the highest ranks.

Josef von Sternberg played a major role in my development. I had really liked *The Blue Angel*, but *Morocco* left me cold—though to be fair, I saw it in a terrible print. Maybe I was too young, too. I watched it again later and found it magnificent, breathtaking in its modernity.

You preferred Vittorio Cottafavi, one of the Italian directors who became a leading figure of Mac-Mahonism, over Michelangelo Antonioni?

I think the first film of his we saw was *Free Women*. I had just returned from the provinces; Michel Fabre came to meet me at the station. We went straight to the Paramount—when it still deserved the name—and were completely dazzled by the film, at least the first half. As often happens with melodramas, the second half gave way to more conventional formulas.

Traviata '53 is a more intimate, more cohesive film—darker and more bitter, too. Then we saw *Milady and the Musketeers* and *Il cavaliere di Maison Rouge*, which confirmed Cottafavi's talent and also showed that a genre film could carry intelligence, subtlety and wit, all of which deepened the sincerity of a hidden emotional core, even when the actors weren't always up to the task.

Our vehemence in defending what we loved could come off as abrasive, or even arrogant, but all we wanted was to push the conversation further, to deepen the thinking around mise en scène and what made cinema specific as an art form. And we kept running into misunderstanding, ignorance—or worse, bad faith.

I never followed Antonioni, certainly not after *La Notte*, which I felt quite alienated from, despite my earlier appreciation for *Le Amiche*, largely due to my affection for the Cesare Pavese novella that inspired it. Even *The*

Passenger, with its celebrated very long final take, left me cold. I love long takes in Preminger, but not because they're long. It's because there's a reason behind them, something that drives them forward.

I had noticed Fellini's *I Vitelloni*, of course, which felt like a natural continuation of Pagliero's *Roma città libera*, written by Ennio Flaiano, but I was disappointed by his subsequent films, which I found sentimental and heavy-handed. Later, though, I was won over by *The Clowns* and *Orchestra Rehearsal*. I had been so put off by his melodramatic, sentimental films that I didn't even bother to see *8½*, the film where his style was said to have shifted. On the other hand, I was dazzled by the tour de force of the highway sequence in *Fellini Roma*. I honestly hadn't thought Fellini capable of such craft, such brilliance. I also liked *Casanova*, however uneven it is, and, of course, *Amarcord*.

Did you hope to build a career in cinema?

I had no ambition, no plan. It was more like: the next book I hadn't read, the next film to be released, the next screening to arrange. I became more and more obsessed — completely taken over by films, theatre, literature — so much so that after graduating from high school, I barely made it to two or three law classes. I basically put my studies on hold because of cinephilia. I got three years of military deferral thanks to my university enrollment, until the Algerian War brought that arrangement to an end.

Did your activities at the Mac-Mahon continue during your military service?

Absolutely. That's when we set up the Cercle du Mac-Mahon. I was posted to the army's film unit, which meant I could go out every evening and had my weekends free. The Cercle included Michel Mourlet, Michel Fabre, Jacques Serguine, Alain Archambault, Marc Bernard and Claude Makovski. Our aim was to organise advance screenings at the Mac-Mahon to showcase films and directors we championed. We invited journalists and critics to attend. The first film we programmed, at the beginning of 1961, was a success: Losey's *The Criminal*.

What was the objective of the Cercle du Mac-Mahon?

Several people came out against Losey, probably worried that giving him recognition might cast a shadow over the filmmakers they supported. We were worried that *The Criminal* might veer into a kind of mannerism, but in the end the film got an absolutely wild reception. The second film presented by the Cercle was Fritz Lang's *The Thousand Eyes of Dr. Mabuse*. On both occasions, Lang and Losey came in person to present their work. We brought them to Paris thanks to audience contributions and the support of sympathetic distributors, and we arranged for them to give a series of interviews, something that hadn't really been done before. The coverage in daily and weekly papers really helped get those films traction in cinemas.

After that, we screened works by Cottafavi, as well as Kubrick's *Dr. Strangelove*, Hawks' *Hatari!*, Ford's *The Man Who Shot Liberty Valance* and *Donovan's Reef*, Walsh's *Esther and the King*, Frankenheimer's *The Manchurian Candidate* and *Seven Days in May*, Cassavetes' *Too Late Blues*, Don Siegel's *Hell Is for Heroes*, and many others.

You place Orson Welles lower than do most film historians.

Citizen Kane is overrated. It's probably a landmark, sure. Making such a personal film in 1940 was still relatively new. And since the silent era, there hadn't really been any figures like Griffith or Stroheim, people clearly seen as auteurs. Apart from Frank Capra and a few others, filmmakers were treated like employees. But the final part of *Citizen Kane* strikes me as highly questionable. Even just on a superficial level, the makeup and Welles' performance as the older Kane are completely over the top. You can tell he hadn't yet lived the experience of old age.

We much preferred *The Magnificent Ambersons*. Was it because Welles had, in his childhood, absorbed something of the time and world depicted in Booth Tarkington's novel? Either way, to me the film reads like a Melvillean take on a supposedly more conventional novel, closer to *Pierre; or, The Ambiguities*, which I had just read in Pierre Leyris' French translation.

In a conversation with Losey, I once mentioned what I saw as a progressive vision in *The Magnificent Ambersons*, and—rare for Welles—a grasp of the totality of the scene that allowed you to really take in the characters in all their complexity. It's a synthesis that you don't find anywhere else in his work. The more Welles moved toward fragmented editing, the less interesting I found him. A film like *Touch of Evil*, often listed as one of his most important, felt bloated to me. I rewatched it recently and it still failed to hold my attention. The same goes for his so-called Scottish version of *Macbeth*.

With Touch of Evil—*a film Welles reportedly lost interest in editing—do you think he ultimately undermined his own work?*

There's a drive toward self-destruction in many artists. I'm not so much thinking of the pioneers, who jumped into filmmaking as a kind of adventure, but rather the second generation, those who had already had time to think deeply about cinema. After *The Magnificent Ambersons*, Welles later created situations where people lost faith in him. *Moby Dick*, which Welles had begun filming on stage in London, where he had also directed the play, was shown to his backer, Louis Dolivet, in fifty-minute fragments. Then suddenly, Welles vanished, leaving the project unfinished. That destructive force, buried deep inside so many other filmmakers too, probably explains the trajectory of some of their careers, as much, if not more, than their particular circumstances. That fault line, that crack, might also explain why some of them had greater sensitivity than others who were merely "competent" and lacked that kind of vulnerability. I was able to visit the set of *The Trial* three times during the shoot in Paris, thanks to Marc Bernard and Claude Othnin-Girard. I remember being struck by an exchange between Welles and Anthony Perkins just before the final setup of a scene. Their connection sparked with incredible speed and intensity which seemed almost electric.

People often accused the Mac-Mahonians of being in bad faith. How do you see it now, looking back?

We weren't disputing the *Cahiers du Cinéma* view that Hitchcock was an auteur developing recurring themes. But what mattered to us wasn't the theme, it was how that theme was expressed through mise en scène. It was the followers of Hitchcocko-Hawksianism, trying to flatter the founders of that line of thinking, who were really being disingenuous. They weren't interested in discovery; they used convoluted arguments to "decode" a film with all this baggage of semiotics and structuralism. I remember a meeting between Jean-Louis Comolli and Howard Hawks. Comolli was going on about the concept of space—not space within the frame like other directors do, but space within space. Hawks had no idea what he was talking about. Some people would ramble endlessly just to justify whatever theory they were pushing. That's how untalented filmmakers could be praised to the skies, while truly gifted, promising directors were ignored or even attacked. You could name a whole list of filmmakers — Francis Ford Coppola, Martin Scorsese, Robert Altman, John Boorman, Jerry Schatzberg — who weren't even acknowledged in *Cahiers* back then. What's regrettable about all that bad faith is that people didn't realise what was really going on. The whole thing was about promoting their filmmaker friends, pushing their own trends, and chasing success — at any cost.

The influence of the Mac-Mahonians could still be felt at Cahiers, *though. What about the September 1960 issue of the magazine, which was devoted to Losey.*

Issue 111 of *Cahiers* was something of an exception. The only people who genuinely wanted it were Éric Rohmer and Jean Douchet. They were insistent that it happen. The issue was handed over to the Mac-Mahon group and, despite a few attempts, there was no interference. Before that, Michel Mourlet had published a few pieces in *Cahiers*, including "On a Misunderstood Art," which laid out our view of what mise en scène really meant. And then came Jean-André Fieschi's write-up of the Losey retrospective at the Cinémathèque in 1962, which reeked of bad faith, clearly written under orders. It was pure servility, designed to flatter the dominant ideology of a few self-appointed gurus.

Starting in 1962, Présence du cinéma *became the main outlet for Mac-Mahonian ideas.*

The magazine was somewhat hesitant in its aesthetic positions, but it had the backing of Alfred Eibel, who had struck up a friendship with Michel Mourlet. Alfred was born in Prague and raised in Vienna, and spoke French and German, which enabled him to become very close to Fritz Lang. He was generous and supported us through some difficult times after we left military service.

What was your relationship with Positif?

It was, and remains, more than cordial. We read it regularly, even if we didn't always share its editorial line. *Positif* was more openly left-wing than *Cahiers*, but I never admired filmmakers for political reasons. When *Cahiers* drifted away from cinema, we found ourselves growing closer to *Positif*.

In a way, we played an important role for the magazine by introducing figures like Jerry Schatzberg, John Boorman, Robert Altman and others, all of whom it supported.

The Mac-Mahonians have often been accused of leaning politically to the right. What were the political orientations of your group?

That rumor—that Mac-Mahonism was a right-wing movement—was born out of gossip, spread by opportunistic newcomers and stirred up by a kind of Savonarola-style guru at *Cahiers*. The Mac-Mahon group, which had been quite tight-knit up until 1962, gradually dispersed. It never had any political agenda. Above all, we were cinephiles. If our Four Aces had any political implication, it would be this: Losey was far more left-leaning than many of the directors *Cahiers* was then championing. The same could be said for Lang, certainly in contrast to Hitchcock. Preminger, though famously tyrannical on set, was deeply liberal in the Anglo-Saxon sense and admired throughout the industry, especially by members of the Hollywood blacklist, who saw in him one of the most honest and principled men in Hollywood.

I remember once discussing this with Serge Daney. I asked him, "Don't you find it odd that the Four Aces were more left-wing than those *Cahiers* was championing at the time?" He replied: "It wasn't a matter of political alignment. It was about clarity"—which, at the very least, acknowledged the integrity of our vision. Daney, I think, felt quite uneasy. As a cinephile, he had initially been close to the Mac-Mahon spirit, and his formative trip to America with Louis Skorecki was practically a Mac-Mahonian pilgrimage. It seems that, in order to join *Cahiers*, he had to if not completely renounce his convictions about certain auteurs, then at least compromise on them.

To return to politics: I voted for the first and last time in my life in 1958, during the referendum in favor of Algerian self-determination. It didn't strike me as any great feat to be among the eleven percent who supported an Algerian Algeria. I was becoming more and more closely connected with filmmakers who had been blacklisted. That stance— above all a romantic one—gradually became a part of who I was. Around me, almost all the Mac-Mahonians shared the same state of mind. I'm well aware that Michel Mourlet, whose intelligence and personal qualities I still admire, later veered to the right and wrote for *Aspects de la France*, but that came well after his essay "On a Misunderstood Art." Those who claimed we were right-wing conveniently overlooked the fact that part of the *Cahiers* team had themselves veered sharply right and written pieces in various magazines defending Lucien Rebatet—alias François Vinneuil—a fascist, collaborationist and antisemitic writer and critic.

I also remember immediately taking issue with Jean Curtelin, who was never a Mac-Mahonian, when he published a muddled article on Walsh in *Présence du cinéma* about *The Naked and the Dead,* implying that Walsh endorsed the worldview of Sergeant Croft, played by Aldo Ray, whereas the film clearly shows him as a warmonger whose professionalism is examined critically. It's the same kind of lazy accusation that was recently aimed at Clint Eastwood for *American Sniper.* Anyone with the "cold gaze" Roger Vailland spoke of would immediately see that the film portrays war as horrorific, and its main character—far from being held up as a hero—descends into pure obsession. A perfect example of ideological blinders. People should go back and read Lu Xun, Bertolt Brecht, Roger Vailland, Alfred Hayes and Simon Leys. In fact, I would love to put together an anthology of their most hard-hitting lines, a collection that would make clear the exact syntax that reveals raw life as being sharp, concise and illuminating.

Do you feel that you had blind spots?

At times we may have contributed to a kind of willful ignorance. Every group prided itself on discovering its own favourite filmmakers, but there was a sort of unspoken consensus. I regret not taking an interest in Anatole Litvak much earlier. Beyond the immense talent he showed—at least in the early part of his career—he was also a fascinating figure. In Capra's wartime propaganda series *Why We Fight*, Litvak's contribution was absolutely crucial. It's no coincidence that the best episode, *The Battle of Russia*, was co-directed by Litvak. He had been on the front lines with the Americans as they broke into Germany to liberate the camps, alongside Robert Capa, Irwin Shaw and Peter Viertel. In a documentary about the Hollywood blacklist—though he himself wasn't on it—actress Jane Wyatt, who had been investigated, said he was the first person to call her and warn her. He probably had a deep love for Paris, but I think the reason Litvak returned to France in the early 1950s, when he was still highly regarded in Hollywood, was that he no longer felt at ease in the atmosphere of McCarthyism and its anti-communist crusade. Like Robert Siodmak, the witch hunts must have reminded him of the antisemitic Europe of 1933. The same was surely true for

John Huston, Orson Welles and Robert Parrish. Almost by chance, I came across a 1932 Litvak film called *Cœur de lilas*, whose storyline could have come from Francis Carco, with a similar poetic power, something I have rarely seen in cinema. In his film *The Sisters*, Errol Flynn plays a weak, morally spineless character, an utterly unexpected role. The film was completely torn apart by critics. One wonders how Litvak must have felt in the face of such abuse.

THE LITTLE SOLDIER: ASSISTANT, PRESS ATTACHÉ, DISTRIBUTOR

What led you to start thinking about directing?

It came to me gradually, almost unconsciously, as certain films opened my eyes and the quiet pressure of earning a living took root. Directing wasn't on my mind at all. I was still reading a lot and had the sense I understood structure, and imagined I might be able to help develop scripts. I jotted down a few ideas—more like very short stories. One of them was based on a Renaissance Italian tale that inspired a Shakespeare play. I regret having destroyed it.

My father worked in a garage, and one of the managers there happened to service the car of Henri Decoin. My father arranged for me to visit the set of Decoin's *La Chatte*, which where I met Michel Deville, who became a friend. Even though I really liked some of Decoin's films, like *La Vérité sur Bébé Donge*, I felt a bit out of my depth. I was probably too young to know how to ask the right questions, especially to someone so reserved and gruff, though you could sense he had a warm heart.

Then I worked as a trainee on Chabrol's *Les Cousins*. The first assistant director was Philippe de Broca, who I got on with very well. I had just a bit more responsibility this time, and the energy on set helped me better understand how Chabrol worked, along with his cinematographer Henri Decaë. That summer shoot was a joy. Claude, Paul Gégauff, Jean-Claude Brialy, Decaë, Alain Derobe, who was learning to use the camera, and Atahualpa Lichy, who had just arrived from Venezuela. I almost became Éric Rohmer's assistant on his first feature, *Le Signe du Lion*, but in the end, union rules got in the way.

You were, however, Jean-Luc Godard's assistant.

Yes. Before leaving for military service in November 1959, I had taken the necessary steps to qualify as a first assistant. I was more assertive when *Breathless* was in preproduction and approached Godard's producer, Georges de Beauregard, directly. When Godard came back from South America, I met him with Paul Gégauff and Daniel Boulanger. Even before he had formally committed to the project, we kept crossing paths. At screenings of Mann or Aldrich films, you might run into Truffaut, Rivette, Chabrol or Godard himself. He visited the set of *Les Cousins* and remembered me as a capable intern.

One day, at the corner of Rue de Berri and the Champs-Élysées, I heard him call out: "Pierre, you know I'm making my first film? I want you as my first assistant." And so, at 23,

I became the youngest first assistant in France, something I'm rather proud of.

A lot has been said about how visionary and disruptive the film supposedly was. It's true that Godard was aiming for something natural and unforced during the shoot, but the film was invented in the editing room. Just look at his earlier shorts; it's already there. People talk a lot about the jump cuts in the film's editing, but it's not like they were planned that way from the start. Godard wanted to shoot in natural light, with no additional lighting, using a new kind of film stock, and the results were uneven. As well as that, the acting could be a little awkward in places, so it was in the editing room that the idea of using jump cuts came up. Every artist learns as they go, and this film, in the end, turned out to be a defining one.

How did military service affect your career as an assistant?

To avoid being sent to the front in Algeria, I gave up my draft deferment in November 1959, just after *Breathless*. If it hadn't been for that twenty-eight-month military service, my life might have taken a different path. Early on during my service, I was contacted by Chabrol's production manager to be first assistant on *Les Godelureaux*, but I had to turn it down. The fact that I had already worked as a first assistant helped me get into the army's film service, with support from Jean Herman—better known under his pen name, Jean Vautrin—whose wife had worked on the editing of *Breathless*. It was a cushy posting that kept me from being sent to the front. All in all, I only spent four days in Algeria, and even that was for a mission that was cut short after a minor debacle involving a Colonel.

In 1961, at the army film service, I directed two totally uninspired military training shorts, and not long after that came up with an original idea for a short film with a bit more substance. It became *La Passe de trois*, which I shot while on leave. I had the idea that I could make two short films back-to-back, and started preparing them together, until, right before the shoot, the producer told me he could only finance one. Michel Deville liked *La Passe de trois* and went on to produce *Les Genoux d'Ariane*, which I co-wrote with Alain Archambault and was built more around the dialogue than it was a formal screenplay. I wanted to make up for the shortcomings of the first film and aimed for greater fluidity in the camerawork. Making *Les Genoux d'Ariane* taught me a lot about lenses and spatial awareness, about where to place the camera, of the spaces around the actors. That's when I began to understand that a sense of rhythm is essential in directing.

Did you return to assistant directing after your military service?

There were a few months of uncertainty when I was still thinking I would continue as an assistant, and to make a bit of money I worked for José Bénazéraf, who was making soft-core porn films. He had a certain charm and was a bit eccentric, but spending a few weeks with him was actually rather fun and colorful. With Alain Derobe, the cinematographer, our main role was helping him scout girls—most of whom never followed up, although to be fair, we didn't exactly encourage them to.

I worked again with Michel Deville, first on a feature, *À cause, à cause d'une femme*, then on a TV film, *Les Petites Demoiselles*, after which I began to move away from assistant directing because I was starting to work as a press agent. That said, if Losey had gone on to make *The Furnished Room* after *Eva*, I would have been his assistant. Fritz Lang would have taken me on too if he had been able to make his final film. He had seen my first two shorts and—out of friendship, perhaps—said he was convinced I had a good sense of composition. His eyesight was beginning to fail, and he told me it would be wonderful to have me by his side—"as if I had a son to whom I could pass on my secrets."

Later on, I became friends with Howard Hawks and traveled with him to Sweden, then to America. We would sometimes have lunch in Paris with actresses he was thinking of bringing to America, like Françoise Dorléac or Romy Schneider. He seemed to trust my judgment and asked me to arrange screen tests for a few European actresses. I picked out about a dozen, including Katrin Schaake, whom Hawks wanted to hire. As I worked with the actresses during rehearsals, I learned to be more responsive. What one actress discovered in a scene might be carried over into the next with another. There was a sense of fullfillment and creative enjoyment in those sessions. I regret misplacing those camera rolls. In terms of performance and continuity, I think they were the best work I ever did in cinema.

How did you become a press attaché?

It happened almost by accident, while I was running the Cercle du Mac-Mahon. Jean-Luc de Carbuccia was a regular there, and his mother, Adry, was a major producer. After a screening of *The 1,000 Eyes of Dr. Mabuse*, Jean-Luc thought he could persuade her to back Fritz Lang's next film, tentatively titled *And Tomorrow: Murder!* As a result, I was brought in to manage the release of Jean Renoir's *Le Caporal épinglé*, which they had produced.

Around the same time, José Giovanni—who seemed to think I had a certain persuasive charm—had co-written the script for *Rififi à Tokyo* with its director, Jacques Deray. He asked me to see the film and, if I liked it, to promote it to the press. I thought it was good, and decided to apply the method I had developed at the Cercle du Mac-Mahon: private screenings and detailed conversations with the director. I wanted to distinguish myself from the usual press attachés, who dealt only in celebrity access and canned interviews with stars. I worked without a press kit. I'm totally against today's approach, where you get bombarded with reams of useless documentation. You've got to work without a net.

I reached out to the critics I knew and screened the film for them personally. It was well received—so well, in fact, that it led to a follow-up: *Symphonie pour un massacre*. Word began to spread, and I found myself in demand. Roger Wasserman and Jacques Maréchal, knowing what I had done for Losey, asked me to take on *The Servant*, which had been badly received by critics at Venice. I gave careful thought to who I should show it to in order to turn things around, and organised one-on-one screenings for each major critic. By the time of the French release, the tide had turned and the press reception was overwhelmingly positive.

Wasserman—later the owner of Le Saint-Séverin cinema and creator of Les Grands Films Classiques with Jacques Maréchal and Jean Gaborit—entrusted me with the re-release of Renoir's *Rules of the Game*. I wouldn't claim to have reintroduced the film; it already had a strong reputation thanks to that restoration. I acted as a kind of conductor, as I did around the same time with the reissue of *King Kong*. You've got to give credit to those people who really loved cinema, who had taste, and who weren't afraid to take risks.

It was in this context that you founded Mac-Mahon Distribution in 1963.

I spoke with Emile Villon, the director of the Mac-Mahon cinema, and suggested that we take charge of distributing certain films ourselves. He agreed, and we ended up releasing a large number of titles that had either never been shown in France or were seriously underrated at the time. Our first release, in 1964, was Losey's *The Damned*, which had never been distributed. That was followed in rapid succession by a series of Raoul Walsh films—*White Heat*, *Colorado Territory*, *Gentleman Jim*, *The Enforcer*—and soon after by works from Sternberg, Tourneur, Hawks, Mann, Fuller, McCarey and La Cava. There were more, but I can't remember them all now.

It was a personal commitment, not just to distribute these films, but to promote them as well. It might seem surprising now, but a film like *The Scarlet Empress* was completely unknown at the time. Its re-release sparked renewed interest in Sternberg, who until then was mostly known for *The Blue Angel*. It also gave me the chance to bring attention to overlooked Raoul Walsh films like *The Man I Love*.

What were the most significant releases from Mac-Mahon Distribution?

One was Samuel Fuller's *Shock Corridor*, a film that had been both a critical and commercial failure in America and which no foreign distributor wanted to take a chance on. I went to the Paris office of Allied Artists to see Ernest Weinstein, a charming old gentleman, and secured the rights without difficulty. The film became an unexpected success in France, reviving Fuller's international reputation. *Shock Corridor*, which had been banned in England, was finally screened there, and in several other countries as well.

Another landmark was Leo McCarey's *Make Way for Tomorrow*. I had met McCarey during my first trip to America. In fact, I may well be the only living cinephile who had the chance to speak with him. I was too young to know how to converse properly, and he was already quite frail. At one point, he sat at the piano and while playing old Irish melodies, spoke—gently, half to himself. When I asked which of his films he most valued, he replied without hesitation: *Make Way for Tomorrow*. He told me Lubitsch had adored it. Winning the Oscar that same year for *The Awful Truth* had disappointed him deeply, he said, because *Make Way for Tomorrow* had failed so completely. By 1964, the film had all but vanished. No one spoke of it. I asked to see it, and it turned out that the only copy in existence was a 16mm print. The film moved me profoundly, and I decided to release it. We programmed it at the Studio de l'Étoile in 1967. It was met with real critical acclaim, though I knew it would be a commercial failure—and it was. The following year, I released another McCarey film, *Ruggles of Red Gap*, which was a triumph, even weathering the unrest of May '68. It drew 170,000 admissions in Paris. By contrast, *Make Way for Tomorrow* had sold only 2,000, so I thought, "Let's bring it back. Out of those 168,000, surely some will want to discover this other film." A miscalculation: it sold just 600 tickets. I suspect the reason lay in the film's subject. Its unflinching portrayal of old age, and the way it forces us to confront the reality of children abandoning their parents, was simply too painful. When a film touches a nerve that raw, audiences sometimes recoil.

Did the Mac-Mahon group's rediscovery of directors neglected in American help them revive their careers back home?

There are two American films from the late 1960s that I'm especially proud to have, in some small way, helped bring about. The first is Abraham Polonsky's *Tell Them Willie Boy Is Here*. His earlier film, *Force of Evil*, had been a resounding failure in the handful of countries where it was even released—essentially nowhere—and had never been shown in France. The only point of reference was a glowing essay by Karel Reisz, which had made Chabrol especially eager to see it. I released it in 1967, and it was warmly received by critics.

I had met Polonsky in 1965. He was already working on the script for *Madigan* for Don Siegel. When I sent him the French reviews of *Force of Evil*, he seized the moment. *Willie Boy* was being developed by Philip Waxman, an independent producer known mostly for having backed Losey's *The Big Night*, but who hadn't done much since.

Martin Ritt, who was riding high at the time, had agreed to direct *Willie Boy*. Abe asked him to hand over the directing duties, and he agreed. Abe then went to Jennings Lang, a top executive at Universal, with the reviews I had sent him, and said: "Look at what I'm getting for a film I made back in 1948. Give me a shot at directing something now and I'll show you I can do even better."

Jennings had an instinct for people. He had taken a chance on Eastwood and Siegel for *The Beguiled*, and on Jerry Schatzberg for *Puzzle of a Downfall Child*. So he said yes to Polonsky.

I offered to screen *Willie Boy* to every director I knew who had ever made a Western. Two of them—John Ford and Raoul Walsh—had to bow out because of their failing eyesight, but they gave me permission to write whatever I wanted and promised they would sign it. Hawks, Vidor,

Dwan, Wellman, Fuller, Lang, Boetticher, Garnett—they all came to a screening I arranged, as did Jim Thompson, Daniel Mainwaring, Adrian Scott, and plenty of others. It was incredibly lively discussing the film with them. I teased the older ones by saying the front office was against the movie, which instantly got them on its side.

The most extraordinary moment came when William Wellman, long considered a staunch conservative, passionately defended the film, rallying Tay Garnett and Allan Dwan with him. Then he picked up the phone and called Lew Wasserman, the head of Universal, who had once been his agent, and told him flatly that he was an idiot for not backing the picture. The next day, Jennings Lang pulled me aside and said, "Pierre, do what you think is necessary, but please, don't let anyone call Lew Wasserman an idiot."

The other film I helped bring to life was Jerry Schatzberg's *Scarecrow*. In 1970, American critics had been merciless toward his debut, *Puzzle of a Downfall Child*, but since I had earned Jennings Lang's trust, he agreed to let me handle distribution and promotion in France, where it got a very warm reception. It came out just before the Cannes Film Festival, where I was looking after Sydney Pollack, who was there with *Jeremiah Johnson*. At the dinners I organised for Sydney, Jerry's name kept coming up in conversations with some of the most influential critics. Sydney was so impressed that when problems arose with Mark Rydell—his producing partner, who had been set to direct *Scarecrow*—he handed the project over to Jerry.

On the other hand, some filmmakers you tried to champion have fallen into obscurity.

Leslie Stevens, for example. I remember the shock and surprise of *Private Property*, a film with a compact intensity, a kind of raw, stripped-down power. That impression was confirmed with *Hero's Island*, which had the same taut, elemental force. Later there was Stan Dragoti's *Dirty Little Billy*, a film that truly deserves to be seen again. It has vanished almost entirely, which is a great shame.

How did you meet Bertrand Tavernier?

I worked alone for about two years, until 1965. As the workload grew, I reached out to Bertrand. I already knew him as a fellow cinephile; he was handling the promotion of Georges de Beauregard's productions at the time, and I suggested that we collaborate. We always got on well. Ours was a friendship rooted in mutual respect, both personal and professional. We supported one another at every turn. We didn't charge large fees; the films we championed were rarely commercial bets. But life was simpler then—less expensive—and we managed. Bertrand had an immense love for cinema, paired with an encyclopedic and deeply felt knowledge. From the 1970s onward, he established himself as one of the central figures in French filmmaking.

How did you divide the work with Bertrand?

We split up certain films based on our tastes and inclinations, but we could always step in for each other when needed. For instance, Bertrand handled the Boetticher films, I looked after *Jeremiah Johnson* and John Boorman's *Leo the Last,* which was a failure everywhere, except in France. I had a good rapport with Ned Tanen, and because of him we took on Miloš Forman's *Taking Off,* which became a success in France. Since I was no longer on good terms with Losey, Bertrand took care of *Accident* in 1967. We had a great understanding, and it was easy for either of us to pick up where the other left off. We also worked on films for French producers or directors who came to us directly. I had really liked *Classe tous risques,* so when Claude Sautet finished *L'Arme à gauche,* he asked me to accompany the film, which ended up being a critical success. Claude called me again for *Les Choses de la vie,* which Bertrand and I worked on together. Jacques Deray was a regular client, and Bertrand brought in Pierre Granier-Deferre, who asked us to handle several of his best films. We also championed Jean-Pierre Melville's *Le Deuxième Souffle.*

You mainly handled English and American films.

We kept close watch on what Hawks and Ford were doing, and brought those directors to France at a time when arthouse cinemas were thriving and there was a passionate audience—much broader than today—which allowed us to do real groundwork, even for films that had been box-office disappointments in America.

The kind of successes we had didn't always endear me to American studio executives, especially when their pessimistic predictions were proven wrong, as was the case with *Puzzle of a Downfall Child.* We also managed to unearth and champion independent films like Leonard Kastle's *The Honeymoon Killers,* which built such a strong reputation in France that it became a full-fledged cult film.

When you look at the inherent quality of these films that didn't work elsewhere, it makes you wonder if the studios ever really knew how to handle them. When Sydney Pollack finished *Jeremiah Johnson*, no one at Warner Bros. believed in it. If Pollack and Robert Redford ever spoke of me with warmth and respect, it's because I "saved" that film. In fact, we had such strong backing from French exhibitors that Boorman's *Hell in the Pacific* and *Puzzle of a Downfall Child* were shown in France in the versions their directors intended and nowhere else.

Back then, the issue of print quality was already a concern. It wasn't just about preserving the films, but also about finding them in their original, uncut versions.

Mac-Mahon Distribution probably came along at just the right time to help preserve certain films in their entirety. The first prints we received of Lang's *Secret Beyond the Door* and Ophüls' *Letter from an Unknown Woman* were each missing about fifteen minutes, cut either for American television or for re-releases in local cinemas in Britain. I immediately contacted Richard Rosenfeld, who held the rights, and told him we needed complete versions. He searched the labs where the cut footage had been stored, recovered the missing scenes, and the films were finally shown in their full original form.

As you began distributing films and handling publicity, the issue also came up—for some films at least—of providing better-quality subtitles.

As a young cinephile, I naturally watched films with subtitles and quickly became aware of their flaws. Little care was taken with timing: subtitles would often straddle two or more shots, breaking the rhythm of the editing. The real turning point came with *The Servant*. There was pressure from both Losey and screenwriter Harold Pinter to ensure that the French subtitles reflected the precision of the dialogue. I took the matter to Jean Perdrix, then head of Cinétitres, and to Nissim Calef. Together, we established a simple but crucial rule: no subtitle should ever span two consecutive shots. We realised that once a subtitle passed a certain character count, it became hard to read, so it was better to break it up to make it clearer and closer to the natural rhythm of speech. We found that you needed at least three frames at the beginning and end of each subtitle to make it readable. I brought in young cinephiles like

Pierre Cottrell, Bernard Eisenschitz and Robert Louit to work on the subtitles for some of the films distributed by Mac-Mahon Distribution. Later, I had an experience that really fascinated me. When I was preparing for the Cannes screening of King Hu's *A Touch of Zen* in 1975, there was no one available to subtitle the Mandarin dialogue, so I asked the writer and sinologist Simon Leys to do the translation. His work was incredibly beautiful, but far too long for the constraints of subtitling. Since I didn't want to condense the text, I had to make choices, keeping only the most striking lines and reluctantly cutting others. Subtitling made further progress with simulation tools that let you overlay subtitles on a video copy and tweak them in real time while watching, to test their accuracy and natural flow. Taking into account a glint in the eye, the tone of a voice, the rhythm of a line, simulation allows for an incredibly fine-tuned result.

Bertrand Tavernier was already an established critic, but aside from your book on Losey, you didn't write very much yourself.

I suppose I was both too lazy and too dissatisfied with what I wrote. Half-hearted, too. Back in school, my essays were always as short as humanly possible. My preferred forms — poems, aphorisms, pamphlets — always made me think that one had a duty to be extremely concise.

You were known for your very hands-on approach with journalists, for being unusually involved in the films you promoted.

We weren't as interventionist as some made us out to be. The critics knew we really knew our cinema. Most of the time, all it took was a phone call to spark someone's interest. Sure, there were times when we pushed critics to their limit, but more often than not, it wasn't necessary. During the Comolli era at *Cahiers du Cinéma*, it was said that Claude Sautet would have been "nothing without the terrorist seduction operations of Rissient and Tavernier." Naturally, we made sure to thank them for the free publicity. But while we had courteous and often friendly relationships with critics, and while we were respected as cinephiles and did our jobs seriously, Claude Sautet would have become Claude Sautet with or without us.

How many films did Mac-Mahon Distribution release in total?

Around seventy, all without a cent of government support. The company was in very good shape, but it worked best in the early years, probably because I was devoting more time and energy to it. And there is also the fact that, once we started having success, a lot of people tried to copy us and flooded the market with films that were often not as good. Telling audiences, "You're about to discover an extraordinary film," works if you're talking about something like *Gentleman Jim* or *Ruggles of Red Gap.* You can do that ten times a year, but when it happens fifty times, people start to lose faith.

Between 1964, when we started, and 1972, costs also went up and we would have needed to find partners to expand the company. I probably could have done that, but at the time what mattered most to me was gaining even more freedom. That independence is probably what kept me young in spirit. Given my relationships with the rights holders, I probably could have built up a film library and gotten into video, something I completely failed to anticipate. I regret that, because it would have made me less poor today. There really should be some kind of flat-rate tax for scouts, what the Americans call a finder's fee.

Your work as a press agent allowed you to bridge the gap between old and new Hollywood, with the generation of filmmakers who took over starting in the late 1960s.

A lot of these filmmakers were just starting out. I had sometimes met them by chance, like Francis Ford Coppola, whom I came across at William Bowers' place. Roger Corman introduced me to Jack Nicholson, Monte Hellman and Martin Scorsese. Jack, in turn, introduced me to Bob Rafelson. I was the first to see some of their films, sometimes even rough cuts, like Scorsese's *Mean Streets.* I would help guide them toward Cannes or find them a distributor in France. I brought *Mean Streets* to the Directors' Fortnight. Robert Favre Le Bret, the president of the Cannes Film Festival, had turned it down for the Official Selection, arguing that Scorsese was unknown.

It would be a stretch to call it a "school," but that generation, which emerged in the late 1960s, was incredibly productive and creative for a few years. It was thrilling to watch films for which I had no frame of reference, no preconceived ideas, whereas reading or watching the great classics can sometimes feel like a chore, because you already think you know them inside out, and that can make them feel a bit dry. I had to let go of the Four Aces and the rest, and engage with these new filmmakers, never knowing which of their films would ultimately stand the test of time. Take someone like Mark Rydell. His first film, *The Fox*, didn't grab me, and *The Reivers* seemed tedious and old-fashioned. And yet, oddly, *The Cowboys*, with John Wayne caught my interest, then *Cinderella Liberty* and *The Rose* confirmed Rydell's talent. I also remember *For the Boys*, which contains an especially powerful scene where James Caan and George Segal are caught up in the blacklist era, and you really feel the pressure that ultimately drives Caan to betray his closest friend. Similarly, I wasn't taken with Rafelson's *Five Easy Pieces*, but his *The King of Marvin Gardens* struck me as a film of startling control and precision.

You had to stay clear-eyed about each filmmaker and each film. Robert Altman, for instance, suffered from a kind of inconsistency that came with his relentless shooting schedule. But I never thought of the filmmakers I liked as part of a movement. New Hollywood or not, it was, above all, auteur cinema. Coppola wasn't so different from the previous generation when he made *The Conversation*. I had fewer dealings with some of the others, probably because I liked their films less. *Goodfellas*, for instance, apart from one inspired scene, seems to me like an attempt to imitate the much stronger *Mean Streets*.

THE DAMNED:
BLACKLISTED FILMMAKERS

Early on—first as a Mac-Mahon cinephile, then as a press agent, distributor and eventually producer—you had close ties with those American directors who had been blacklisted during the McCarthy-era anti-communist purge.

It began with my fascination for Jules Dassin's *Night and the City*. He wasn't working anymore, and that puzzled me. I didn't yet know what the blacklist was. The papers announced that Dassin was coming to France to make *L'Ennemi public numéro un*, with Fernandel and Zsa Zsa Gabor, but when Gabor refused to shoot because of Dassin, the project was handed to Henri Verneuil and eventually released in 1953. Then came *Rififi*, and with it, a growing awareness of Dassin's story and the fate of others who had been accused of communist sympathies and cast out of Hollywood. At the same time, I discovered *The Prowler*, a remarkable film by Joseph Losey, which had a much more complex structure than what we were used to seeing. I noticed the name Hugo Butler in the credits; he had also written *He Ran All the Way*, directed by John Berry. What we didn't know then was that Dalton Trumbo, who had also been blacklisted and sentenced, had co-written both those scripts.

What drew you to these blacklisted artists?

There was definitely a kind of romanticism on my part, a feeling for the persecuted, for artists who had been stripped of their means of expression. Brecht's plays *The Exception and the Rule* and *Man Equals Man* had a big impact on how I came to see the work of the blacklisted writers. In 1953, I was completely taken with Brecht. Around that same time, I started watching Losey's films because I learned that back in 1947 he had directed Brecht's *Life of Galileo* in Los Angeles. In *The Prowler*, I saw a new, deeper, more subtle way of approaching characters, a complex, ambiguous way of breaking them down, and of dealing with the full political, economic and social reality of America at the time. Even Losey's *The Boy with Green Hair* struck me as a Brechtian film. Brecht himself could have written that line delivered by Gramp, one of the main characters played by Pat O'Brien: "There's nothing in the night you can't see in the day." There's also something very Brechtian in how the film gets across a basic truth: directly, clearly, powerfully, and in a way that sticks. For example, when the teacher asks how many blond boys are in the class, a few hands go up; then how many have brown hair, then red hair, and finally, how many have green hair, and Dean Stockwell raises his hand alone. That's a scene that says so much about racism.

Postwar American cinema was heavily influenced by neorealism, and most of the filmmakers leaned left. Brecht had ties to some of them. When you look at the way a screenplay like *Pride of the Marines*, written by Albert Maltz and directed by Delmer Daves, is constructed, or those by Abraham Polonsky, you can't help but feel dialectical materialism at work. There's a way of analysing and synthesising a scene, always in relation to the character and to the broader story.

At the time, I was also immersed in the writings of Roger Vailland, a former Communist, and when I finally grasped what the blacklist meant, I couldn't help feeling a certain sympathy for the humanist ideals of communism, the very ideals for which people like Dassin, Losey and Berry were being persecuted. In Paris, I met writers and screenwriters like Ben Barzman, Paul Jarrico, Michael Wilson and Arnaud d'Usseau, all victims of McCarthyism. John Huston, Anatole Litvak and Robert Siodmak—though Siodmak himself was never under suspicion—were all at the height of their careers and came to Europe because they couldn't stand the atmosphere in Hollywood.

Can we imagine what the films of these American directors and screenwriters exiled in Europe and France might have looked like if they had been able to stay in America?

If silent-era comedy directors like Monta Bell, Clarence Badger and Malcolm St. Clair had made the transition to talkies alongside Lubitsch, McCarey and La Cava, they would have carried over that same elegance and refined charm that made their earlier films so special. And if the blacklist had never happened—if Dassin, Losey, Berry and Endfield had stayed in America—their work would surely have grown richer. But just as importantly, the creative cross-pollination with other filmmakers might have inspired those others to push themselves further. Maybe that generation could have driven a kind of artistic progress in America, something imagined by utopians and romantics, not businessmen.

Among those you met, Cy Endfield stood apart as being more guarded and elusive.

Cy Endfield was an intriguing figure. As a young man, he was the most famous magician in America, and when he later drifted away from cinema after a string of commercial flops, he had enough advanced knowledge of mathematics to design a kind of early pocket computer, which was way ahead of its time. Sadly, his health declined and he was never able to bring it to market. His films were deeply leftist. Take *Inflation*, a short he made for MGM, which starred Edward Arnold, well known as the villain in Capra's comedies, as a craven banker taking direct orders from Hitler to spark an economic crisis in America that would serve Nazi interests. The film was pulled after just one day, despite having opened on five hundred screens. How such a film was ever greenlit at MGM, the most conservative of the major studios, is baffling.

Inflation likely planted the seed for Endfield's *The Argyle Secret*, which began as a radio play and became a lean, low-budget thriller about wartime profiteers and traitors, a theme it treated with startling directness. How did a film like that, released only in second-tier theaters, manage to take on such a loaded subject? Then Endfield made a major film: *The Sound of Fury*. Taken together with *The Underworld Story*, these four films form a body of work arguably more radical than the combined output of Dassin, Losey and Berry.

In France, Endfield remains largely unknown, remembered mainly for Zulu, *his greatest commercial success, made when he was exiled in Britain.*

Cy was actually very active in England, making several ultra-low-budget films. I'm one of the lucky few who's seen *The Secret*, a very unusual film he made at the start of his exile. It's a mystery how it even got financed, considering the lead actor, Sam Wanamaker, was also blacklisted. The British production company had no real hope of releasing the film in America.

I met Endfield through Stanley Baker. Among the blacklisted community, he was spoken of with some bitterness. He had divorced a wife who was well liked among them, and that, for some, was enough to cast him out. In England, he married a young woman—just 18 when they met—and lived a modest, almost reclusive life. In 1960, perhaps out of exhaustion, or in search of better working conditions, he made the difficult decision to appear before the House Un-American Activities Committee. I admire Cy enormously, but I can't defend that. It didn't help his standing with the anti-communists, and it led to him being shunned by many of the blacklisted circle.

He later made *De Sade*, which flopped, despite having real merit, and then *Universal Soldier*, which had a promising early script. But Cy had to lower his expectations when he was forced to cast George Lazenby in the lead — a weak replacement for Sean Connery as James Bond in *On Her Majesty's Secret Service*.

Paul Jarrico had been a friend of Endfield's since their school days, and I had the pleasure of reuniting them many years later. Paul was then living between Paris, Prague and London. Of all those targeted by HUAC, he was the first to make peace with Cy. The circumstances of Jarrico's death in 1997, when he was 82, were especially tragic. He died in a car accident just two days after several unions that had spent fifty years justifying the blacklist finally came out and condemned it. For years, Paul had been the driving force behind the effort to restore proper screenwriting credits to blacklisted writers. As the press noted, he never pushed to get his own credits reinstated, saying that he had time on his side — unlike some others. Back when he was doing card tricks and magic shows off-Broadway, Cy was brought in by Jarrico as a technical advisor on a film with Abbott and Costello, *Little Giant*, directed by William A. Seiter, which needed a magician's touch. Around that same time, Orson Welles had just finished *Citizen Kane*, and hearing that Cy was in Hollywood, he asked to meet him because he wanted to learn a few tricks. Cy agreed, but asked in return to learn about filmmaking. Welles got him hired as an assistant to Jack Moss on *The Magnificent Ambersons*. Cy was present at the film's two test screenings, when it still ran two hours and fifteen minutes. According to him, it was brilliant from beginning to end. He was convinced that if Welles had returned from South America — where he was shooting *It's All True* — he would have had the final say on the edit. Maybe not the full two hours and fifteen, but certainly something much longer than the cut we know today, with its heavy edits and added scenes. It just goes to show, if it needed proving, how Welles squandered a lot of goodwill from producers who had genuinely believed in him.

You knew John Berry well. Your relationship began with He Ran All the Way, *when it screened at the Mac-Mahon, and extended all the way to* Boesman and Lena, *his final film, which you produced. Curiously, despite having lived in France, he remains little known there.*

In 1940, John acted in *Native Son*, Richard Wright's adaptation of his own novel, directed by Orson Welles, and when the production went on a national tour, John took over as director. It was a major success but provoked outrage in parts of America. The *Citizen Kane* press baron himself, William Randolph Hearst, had his newspapers attack the show repeatedly. The second major link between John and the black community came with the play *Deep Are the Roots* by Arnaud d'Usseau and James Gow. It had originally been staged by Elia Kazan, but John again took over for the national tour, with Betsy Blair and James Edwards in the lead. His staging featured what was, at the time, a first on the American stage: a black man kissing a white woman. The play caused quite a stir—again. Later, in New York, he directed *Les Blancs*, and I was lucky enough to see it. The staging struck me as both fluid and remarkably layered. Cameron Mitchell—who appeared in many films in the 1950s and had never especially impressed me—was outstanding in that production.

In the 1960s, John also directed Athol Fugard's *Blood Knot* in London and then in New York, where it was a triumph. That was followed in 1970 by *Boesman and Lena*, Fugard's powerful play about an outcast couple living under apartheid. It ran for eighteen consecutive months in the same theatre. On the strength of that, John was brought back to America to direct *Claudine*, about the struggles of a couple in Harlem. Diana Sands—who was originally cast but had to step down due to illness—so admired John that she insisted on him as director, even though at the time the politically correct choice would have been to hire an African American director. In the 1980s, John also staged Fugard's *Hello and Goodbye in Paris* in a beautiful production, though sadly in a theatre that was far too small.

For years, I tried to help get one of John's films off the ground. He had a project in the same spirit as his 1955 film *Ça va barder*, a mix of dark humor and offbeat fantasy, about two gangsters returning home. He wrote two drafts— both rich in detail, with vivid scenes—but could never quite pull them into shape. It didn't help that his career, spread out over many years, across different countries, and moving between theater, film and television, made him hard to pin down for people in the industry. He had a brief window to do a new take on Boris Vian's *I Spit on Your Graves*. Vian had known John and had toyed with the idea of letting him do the first version, but by the time a bunch of clueless kids ended up with the rights, the whole thing fell apart.

Despite the promise he showed with Tension *and especially* He Ran All the Way, *Berry never fulfilled his early potential.*

Why do you think that was?

John's politics, his restlessness, his refusal to manage his career—he was the opposite of someone like Losey. He was undisciplined, too willing to chase easy money and women. He's a striking example of someone whose creative drive went beyond the boundaries of his generation, his background, his upbringing. Even in his later years, John didn't grow old in the usual sense. He kept his enthusiasm, his sharp wit, his sense of wonder, and kept evolving in how he saw the world. He stayed close to his Marxist ideals but had shed any trace of didacticism. His passion for current events, his fierce hunger for justice, could be truly startling. I remember one morning when he read in the *International Herald Tribune* about a death sentence in Pakistan: a poor, illiterate boy had handed out flyers in a mosque— clearly manipulated by others—and the government had condemned him to death. John was shaken to the core, and all he could think about was how to save him.

Aside from his intimate knowledge of the African American community, what made him the best director to adapt Boesman and Lena *for the screen?*

I spent a year and a half focused on making *Boesman and Lena* happen. It was a play that John understood on a deep, instinctive level—he saw all its richness, its humanity—and I believed it was a film that could be made on a modest budget. He wanted it to carry the feeling of a world just beginning, especially in the relationship between the first man and the first woman. A kind of miniature, seen under a microscope, with the entire cosmos swirling around it. His adaptation took me by surprise. A text that might seem dry on the surface revealed an extraordinary depth. It came from the way John could shape the rhythm of the lines in ways you didn't expect. He brought enormous weight to the drama, giving it sensuality and a real sense of place. His film version reaffirmed what audiences had felt when the play was first staged in 1970. During casting, the passion of the actresses was incredibly moving, especially two who had played the role years earlier on stage and, though now too old to reprise it, insisted on meeting the man who had brought the play to life again. At that time, Athol Fugard was in New York performing *The Captain's Tiger*, a play about his first voyage at sea as a young deckhand. After the show, John asked to meet him. Fugard came out with his cast and said: "This is my mentor and my master. Without him, I could never have written the way I do, understood what theatre really is, or known, even in the writing, how to bring my plays to life."

I'm still very proud of *Boesman and Lena*. It was a film I really wanted to make. I wanted to see for myself what so many friends still remembered with such awe, thirty years after the play's original production. And I carry with me one of the most vivid memories of my life: John, François Ivernel and I met Danny Glover at dawn during a layover at Roissy, on his way from Ouagadougou back to America. In the deserted lobby of the Hyatt, John laid out his vision of the play — what the role meant, what Lena represented. And it was as if we could see, in close-up, the entire emotional architecture of the film coming to life on Danny's face, in his eyes, with John's voice narrating offscreen. It was stunning — alive with poetry, clarity, urgency. John died before the film was fully edited, but his son Dennis and I made sure it remained completely his. You can't help but think about what he might have achieved, had he not been shut out by the blacklist or had he managed his career, and his body of work, with a little more discipline.

And yet you might be surprised, for example, to know just how much Edward Yang — the Taiwanese filmmaker — admired John. As soon as he got to Paris, he would rush to have dinner with him at the Zéphyr. He was completely captivated by John's vitality, his laughter, his uncompromising vision of the world.

When you were a publicist, you had the chance to work with other blacklisted filmmakers.

Bertrand and I got a huge amount of pleasure — and pride — working on Herbert Biberman's *Slaves* at Cannes in 1969. When I was younger, I hadn't much liked *Salt of the Earth*, which I found too preachy. That was a pretty narrow view, especially considering the film was made with no money, no proper equipment, and under FBI surveillance. Maybe I came to sympathise more with the blacklisted filmmakers over time. Or maybe I just grew up a bit. In any case, when I saw the film again later, I appreciated it much more, and found it surprisingly modern, both in terms of aesthetics and the way it tackled social issues.

Biberman had an incredible energy and drive and a real social conscience, which is rare. Everyone was taken aback by the complexity of Stephen Boyd's slave owner character in *Slaves* and by Boyd's performance. I would take that film, with all its naivety, any day over the more self-conscious one Steve McQueen directed, *12 Years a Slave*.

When Dalton Trumbo made *Johnny Got His Gun*, based on his own novel, Herbert told him he absolutely had to hire Bertrand and me because we had stuck by *Slaves* so loyally. One day, Herbert more or less dragged me out to see *Coming Apart*, a film by someone no one had heard of called Milton Moses Ginsberg. I was surprised Herbert liked it, but it just goes to show: the more open your mind is, the more it soaks up, the more it grows. I met Ginsberg later on and I really think he's one of those filmmakers who never got the career they deserved. He was a terrific editor and had a great ear for dialogue too.

Of all the blacklisted filmmakers, Joseph Losey is the one you had the most complex relationship with. You wrote the first book about him, which is the only book you ever wrote. And yet, both the man and the filmmaker kept somehow disappointing you.

When I was very young, I believed that an artist was someone who stood up for certain values. I never even asked myself whether they lived up to the values in their work. But it's possible to believe in something, even dedicate yourself to it, without actually living by it. Losey was the first person who made me realise that.

As I mentioned, I first met him around the time of *Time Without Pity*, a film we campaigned for. Because the release was so delayed in France, by the time it came out his film *Blind Date* was already finished. It opened the Cercle du Mac-Mahon. That film wasn't as strong as the previous one, but it actually got a warmer reception from audiences. *The Criminal*, which came along soon after, disappointed us, but this time the critics loved it almost unanimously. Within a few months, Losey was established in the minds of the critics, and he was offered *Eva*. As I said, if I hadn't been doing my military service, I would have been his assistant on that shoot.

As it happened, I saw the film for the first time in Munich, with Fritz Lang. Conrad von Molo was in charge of the German dubbing. We watched a different cut — slightly longer and with different music — than the one we know today. One scene had Billie Holiday singing "Yesterday" while Stanley Baker prowled around Jeanne Moreau's apartment. The producers couldn't get the rights, so they had to switch it out, after which it was as if the film had lost its secret choreography. Something almost magical was now missing.

There were a few things about *Eva* that bothered us, even if we didn't want to admit it at the time, overwhelmed as we were by the film's power. There was something original about it, something vulnerable and deeply personal, that still stands out. Later, with *King and Country*, I began to feel that Losey was guilty of a certain snobbishness, of trying to please the intelligentsia. One thing, I think, explains how Losey's personality evolved. Because of his background and education, he had an aristocratic temperament, and he liked to present himself that way. I remember once he dismissed the name of Cy Endfield with a wave of his hand, like a patrician brushing off a commoner. He was probably annoyed by the friendship between Endfield and Stanley Baker, and definitely jealous of Endfield's paycheck, which was much higher than his. Not so much because of the money itself, but because of what the gap in status implied.

Was King and Country *the moment when you came to understand that Losey wasn't the man you had idealised?*

Even before that film, I knew that Losey hadn't always behaved very honourably, at least not with a couple of friends: Adrian Scott, who gave him his break by producing *The Boy with Green Hair*, and Daniel Mainwaring, who fought to get him hired as the director of *The Lawless*. The producers had originally wanted Irving Reis, but Mainwaring pushed for Losey, who at the time was just a screenwriter at MGM. Harry Kruger had asked Mainwaring to write a script for Losey to direct. It wasn't much of a script, true, but the way he found out he had been replaced was brutal. Waking up groggy from surgery, still under the fog of anesthesia, he was told by Kruger that George Tabori had taken his place.

After the commercial failure of *Eva*, Losey signed on to adapt *The Most Dangerous Game*, a Série noire crime novel by Gavin Lyall. The producer was meant to be Adrian Scott, who had finally come off the blacklist and been hired by MGM in London. Scott even got Warren Beatty to agree to the project. But then Losey had a surprise hit with *The Servant*, which he had shot in the meantime, and suddenly he felt he was above doing studio assignments. He pulled out of the contract, and Adrian Scott was sent back into the wilderness. Later on, when Hugo Butler became seriously ill, Trumbo and Robert Aldrich reached out to all their old blacklist friends, asking for contributions to help with medical costs. Losey wasn't exactly stingy, but he didn't give a cent, claiming something about offshore taxes and God knows what else. Trumbo was furious and let him have it in no uncertain terms. And then came *King and Country*, which confirmed for me that Losey was trying, rather clumsily, to ingratiate himself with the fashionable, artsy crowd. On top of that, the book I had published about him around that time didn't sit well with him because in it I expressed some doubts about the direction his work was taking. I can understand why it upset him.

Over time, how did those on the blacklist respond to Soviet politics?

Many were shaken by the Hungarian uprising. Some kept clinging to their illusions, others faced it head-on, like John Berry. He saw how the French left—his own friends— reacted, and how they refused to acknowledge what was really happening. That was actually the theme of *The Way of the World*, the play by Ted Allan—who had once been Norman Bethune's secretary—which in London in 1958 John directed, produced and acted in. We later tried to adapt it into a film.

Losey, on the other hand, remained a Stalinist. Herbert Biberman took a while to wake up. Sidney Buchman, who was living in exile in France, came to terms with it more quickly, partly because he had already begun to distance himself from communist ideology. He was the only one who testified and said, "Yes, I was a member of the Communist Party from such-and-such year to such-and-such year. I'm not anymore. But don't ask me to name names. I won't do that." Buchman, Biberman and Albert Maltz came from what you might call a kind of American Jewish aristocracy. A lot of the blacklisted writers were Jewish. Of course, what stood out above all was their Marxism, their humanism, their intelligence and their sense of humor. They were highly educated and could write quickly—and well. They knew how to tell a story, they had an ear for dialogue, and they almost instantly became screenwriters. When people asked Ring Lardner Jr. why he became a Marxist at 20, he used to say: "Because the Marxists were way more interesting than the non-Marxists. And it was a great way to meet girls."

Did you ever try to meet people like Edward Dmytryk or Elia Kazan, who gave names to the House Un-American Activities Committee?

I once found myself at a dinner with Don Siegel, sitting next to Richard Collins. I had no idea at the time that he had been an informant. I had really liked his script for *Riot in Cell Block 11*, which Siegel directed, and that's all we talked about. I also came into contact with Kazan through Anatole Dauman, when I was advocating for Lino Brocka. Kazan's public support for Brocka's *Bayan Ko* was invaluable in dealing with the Philippine authorities. His name carried weight. He loved the film, so I met him and we had a very stimulating conversation. Of course I was aware that he had informed, but I didn't bring it up. That said, Kazan's behaviour never stopped me from watching his films, even if I don't share the enthusiasm of those who idolise him. I rewatched *Splendor in the Grass* recently and liked it a lot more than I had the first time. But I still don't think he's the great filmmaker some make him out to be. You might be surprised to hear this, but I often find the acting in his films exaggerated, artificial, even hollow. It doesn't really reveal the characters, it just flattens them into type, especially Brando. And *America, America* is wildly overrated.

THE GOLD SEEKER: THE CANNES FESTIVAL SCOUT

How did your first Cannes Film Festival in 1964 unfold?

It was a pretty unique experience, nothing like the ones I'd had before—or would have later. By 1964, I had already made a bit of a name for myself professionally, but I had never been to Cannes. Two friends of mine—the two people who had introduced me to Beauregard, Henri Lange, who I met during my time in the army's film unit, and Gilbert Wolmark, had started a small foreign sales company and had connected with an Indian actor, Sunil Dutt, who was a huge star at the time. He produced his own films, and one of them, *Mujhe Jeene Do*, had been selected for the competition. Henri and Gilbert invited me to come down to Cannes with them, especially since Fritz Lang was heading the jury that year.

We had no illusions about the Indian film winning anything, but Lang was delighted I would be there to help him out, since his eyesight was poor, and also just to chat. I introduced him to Sunil Dutt and his wife Nargis, a major Bollywood star. The opening film was *The Fall of the Roman Empire*, which was a total flop, although Lang defended it, saying Anthony Mann really had an eye for visuals. Still, the film he liked best was *Vidas Secas* by Nelson Pereira dos Santos.

I also used the opportunity to meet people from abroad, like Charles Champlin, the *Los Angeles Times* critic. Back then, there were very few Americans coming over, and I happened to know some of them, so I was more than happy to show them around.

Which films did you bring to Cannes as a press officer and distributor?

In 1967, Sidney Safir—then the sales agent for British Lion, a major British outfit—asked me to represent Karel Reisz's *Morgan: A Suitable Case for Treatment*. My reputation in London was beginning to solidify as I had already handled Clive Donner's *Nothing But the Best* and *The Caretaker*. Bertrand Tavernier was also at Cannes that year. In 1968, I took on Forman's *The Firemen's Ball*. Miloš knew my work on his Czech films and had specifically asked for me to handle that film. But this was May '68, which, in hindsight, turned out to be a naive utopia for some and just a passing trend for others. Still, it had unfortunate consequences for this young filmmaker from a Soviet satellite state. Two extremely famous French directors showed up and pressured Miloš to withdraw his film from the competition, supposedly in solidarity with the revolution, when in fact he was on the verge of winning the Palme d'Or. He reluctantly agreed. Luckily, Miloš' future in cinema turned out to be a lot more real than the revolution dreamed up in the spirit of May '68, especially considering that one of those two French directors later betrayed that very spirit.

In the early 1970s, you moved beyond your role as a press agent and became more involved in programming at Cannes.

I had already crossed paths with Robert Favre Le Bret, the festival director at the time, but we hadn't really formed much of a relationship. When he became president of the Festival in 1972, he brought in Maurice Bessy—a true cinephile—as general delegate. Bessy asked if I would suggest any films I came across that might interest him. That was the year I helped bring *Jeremiah Johnson* and *The Panic in Needle Park* to Cannes, where both were big hits. That gave me a bit more credibility with Bessy, which is how I managed, in 1975, to push through King Hu's *A Touch of Zen*, even though we only had forty minutes of what was originally a three-hour film. When I first saw it, I was absolutely hooked and was determined to get it into Cannes. But the original version had to be reassembled because no complete copy existed. Taiwanese cinema was completely unknown in Europe at the time, as was King Hu, so it meant really championing the film from a standing start. But just the fact that I was working on it sparked interest from distributors, including Claude Berri, for whom I had also handled *The Firemen's Ball*, and they started lining up to buy it. The film ended up being scheduled fairly late in the competition, which gave me time to act as its ambassador on the Croisette. It got some rave reviews, but also a lot of resistance, and eventually won the Grand Prize from the CST [Commission Supérieure Technique de l'Image et du Son]. It wasn't a major award, but it did make waves in Asia. And it made me think: if a hidden masterpiece like *A Touch of Zen* could be uncovered in Asia and revealed at Cannes, then surely there were other films elsewhere just waiting to be discovered.

In 1971, your ability to get a film into Cannes and give it real visibility was already clear with Johnny Got His Gun.

I had gone to Los Angeles to oversee the subtitling while Trumbo was finishing the final cut, but Favre Le Bret had rejected it. I really believed in the film, so I went to see Jean Renoir, who sent a telegram to Favre Le Bret saying:

"You MUST show this film." Favre called me to say he still wouldn't budge. Then we found out that Buñuel had once been considered to direct the film, so we reached out to him and asked if he would watch it. He replied that he didn't need to; he told us we could go ahead and send whatever telegram we liked. Eventually, Favre Le Bret gave in, but only allowed a single screening, which was a first in the history of the Festival. And yet, that year the film went on to win the Special Jury Prize, tied with Miloš Forman's *Taking Off*, which I also happened to be handling!

In 1973 you brought Scarecrow, *which won the Palme d'Or, and in 1974 Francis Ford Coppola's* The Conversation, *which also made it to Cannes and won the Palme. Did you have a method for getting these films noticed by the press and the jury?*

You can't separate *Scarecrow*'s success at Cannes from the excitement in Paris around Jerry Schatzberg's previous films: *Puzzle of a Downfall Child* and *The Panic in Needle Park*. I had a feeling—and Robert Sherman, the producer of *Scarecrow* and Sydney Pollack's associate, agreed—that Jerry's next film had a good shot at being selected. When I saw the long version, it was clear: this was the one. Warners, which already trusted me after *Jeremiah Johnson*, didn't push back, even though they had more faith in Lindsay Anderson's *O Lucky Man!* The film was ready two months before Cannes and we had already locked in a release date to coincide with the festival. I organised several screenings in Paris, and the French press loved it. We arrived at Cannes with that buzz behind us, which played a big role in its winning the Palme d'Or. People have forgotten *The Hireling* by Alan Bridges, which shared the prize that year. That was also the year of *La Grande Bouffe* by Marco Ferreri and Eustache's *The Mother and the Whore*.

    The Conversation was completed at the last possible moment, and Coppola, through his right-hand man Fred Roos, asked me to shepherd the film. If I hadn't agreed and pushed for it, he and Roos probably wouldn't have sent it to Cannes at all. They sped up postproduction, but I didn't have the chance to set up a Paris screening, and officially I wasn't even handling the film. Some people at the American studios were starting to get a bit touchy about the success of films they hadn't really backed in the first place.

After your frequent trips to Asia in the late 1970s, you returned to Cannes in 1979 to work on Apocalypse Now.

Gilles Jacob, who had just taken over as Cannes' general delegate in 1978, told me that Coppola wanted me to see *Apocalypse Now*. He wanted my opinion on whether it was a good idea to present it at Cannes, and within three days I flew out of Paris, stopped over in Houston, then on to San Francisco. They drove me to the Napa Valley, where Coppola had his vineyard, and I watched the film very late one night—a version pretty close to what would screen two or three weeks later. I stayed the night, had breakfast with Coppola the next morning, flew back to San Francisco, then on to New York to meet with the financiers, and finally took the Concorde back to Paris. It was an adrenaline rush, to say the least.

I was blown away by the film and agreed to take it on. Coppola was at the height of his fame, and the film had originally been expected back in 1976, so the anticipation was monumental. When it came time to show it to the critics, I played it cool and hinted that they shouldn't be surprised, and said we would talk afterward. I knew some would love it and others might reject it, but I figured the whole event could work in our favor. On the day of the screening in competition, we held a selective press preview that went extremely well, and when the official screening happened a few hours later at the Palais, the audience was already buzzing.

Yet the Palme d'Or sparked controversy. Françoise Sagan, who was jury president and had wanted Volker Schlöndorff's The Tin Drum *to win the prize on its own, later claimed that she had been pressured into awarding a joint Palme. Were you aware of the controversy at the time?*

I got the sense that Jules Dassin, who was on the jury, sided with Sagan. If *The Hireling*, which shared the Palme with *Scarecrow* in 1973, has since faded from memory, the battle in 1979 is still remembered. Sagan said there had been pressure. Of course, for Favre Le Bret, it was important that such a major film as *Apocalypse Now* didn't leave empty-handed. But did he actually apply pressure? In the 1990s, when Ciby 2000 won three Palmes d'Or, for *The Piano*, *Secrets & Lies* and *Taste of Cherry*, I can confidently say I played a major part in those wins. But I can also say that there was never any maneuvering or scheming involved. I later handled the Oscar campaign for *The Tin Drum*, just as I had done for Marcel Ophuls' *The Sorrow and the Pity*.

How much did you earn from the films you handled at Cannes?

I did a lot of it for free. If I earned anything from Oshima's *In the Realm of the Senses*, it was just enough to qualify me for France's *intermittence du spectacle*, the unemployment benefits system for freelance artists, which allowed me to scrape by for a while. When I saw Lino Brocka's *Insiang* in Manila, I was stunned. All that mattered to me was that the film be recognised for what it was. I took care of it for nothing, just like I did with *A Touch of Zen* and the films of Lester James Peries.

If I had only done things for money, they simply wouldn't have happened. In fact, I even invested my own funds in some projects. A lot of friends were worried about me, about my retirement, but I didn't give it a thought. After *Scarecrow* in 1973, I was barely earning more than I had in 1960, whether it was for small films or big ones. What mattered most was the work, the films I loved. Ray Stark was so pleased with what I had done for John Huston's *Fat City* that he offered me an extravagant sum to work on *Funny Lady*, the Barbra Streisand sequel which, needless to say, I turned down.

It was clear the studios often didn't recognise their best films. I later found out that some of the people who came into PR after me were making more than I ever earned for *Scarecrow* or *Jeremiah Johnson*, so for *Apocalypse Now*, I asked for more than the usual PR salary, because by then I felt I had proven just how much my work was worth.

When Gilles Jacob became general delegate of Cannes in 1978, he began inviting you to certain screenings.

I travelled to America with Gilles quite a few times. My "payment," so to speak, was a round-trip business class ticket, and around 1984, I officially joined the festival selection committee. My areas were mainly America, Australia and Asia. One of the first discoveries I made was Jane Campion. I had been on the radar of the Australian Film Commission ever since I brought Ken Hannam's *Sunday Too Far Away* to Cannes in 1975, which helped kick off the revival of Australian cinema. Then in 1976 came *The Devil's Playground*, and in 1978 *The Chant of Jimmy Blacksmith*, both by Fred Schepisi, and in 1979 Gillian Armstrong's *My Brilliant Career*, which introduced Judy Davis. I asked to see student films, which is how I came across Campion's early shorts. There was also an Australian filmmaker, Bill Bennett—I brought two of his films to Cannes. Bill didn't quite live up to all the promise, but *Backlash* (1987) did leave its mark. And later, of course, there was Rolf De Heer. Hugely talented, though he never really got the recognition he deserved.

In some cases, getting the films accepted wasn't easy. Peries' *The Mansion by the Lake* should have been given more prominence. If I ever used my influence at Cannes when I was still involved, it was only ever to try and right the many wrongs I saw. But some ill-intentioned people got in Gilles Jacob's ear and told him I shouldn't be on the selection committee anymore because of my "double role" and in 1999 he asked me to step down. We stayed on good terms and he told me I was the first to recommend Thierry Frémaux to him, who I had met through Bertrand Tavernier.

What was your main criterion as a Cannes selector?

Before anything else, I need to feel that a film is well made. By that, I mean the essentials of mise en scène are there. I like films that have a point of view, a distinct voice. I have always trusted my instinct, my eye, or at least the eye I believe I have. I follow my gut. That afternoon in Sydney, when I saw Jane Campion's shorts, it was like being struck by lightning. I instantly sensed there was an auteur, a body of work in the making. I didn't have to think it over; it was as obvious to me as Preminger, Mizoguchi or Ida Lupino had been thirty years earlier.

Discovering Jane Campion must have put you in a strange position in Australia. You were treated like a messiah over there.

It led to some absurd situations. Lots of young women wanted to be the next Jane Campion. One day I was taken to a screening where a young director and her producer sat beside me. After the film, the director turned to me and asked, quite innocently:

"So?"

"It was very interesting and I thank you for showing it to me."

"So you're selecting the film for the festival?"

"I don't select films myself. I can only recommend them to the committee."

"And will you recommend it?"

"I don't want to upset you, which is why I'm telling you now. You're clearly talented and ambitious, but I don't think this film would be accepted. Let's talk about the next one."

"But don't you think this film has great sensitivity? My film bleeds with sensitivity!"

That kind of reaction was pretty common, but I can honestly say I've never done anything out of calculation. I have always relied on spontaneity, instinct and the benefit of a lifetime of experience.

That same instinct led you to spot Reservoir Dogs *and bring it to Cannes in 1992.*

Reservoir Dogs comes out of a tradition of great film noir, definitely a genre I had a solid frame of reference for. You always approach the characters more through their physicality than their intellect. And even when a film is considered "intellectual," I still believe cinema has to be physical.

Before talking about Tarantino, I want to say something about Harvey Keitel, who I first saw in *Mean Streets*. He was just as remarkable in it as Robert De Niro, though De Niro got more of the attention. Harvey was also excellent in *Alice Doesn't Live Here Anymore*, Scorsese's next film. When Bertrand Tavernier was preparing *Death Watch*, he mentioned he wanted to cast Harvey. I thought it was a great idea and helped put them in touch. In *Bad Lieutenant*, which came out just before *Reservoir Dogs*, Harvey was extraordinary. He was the one who told me about Tarantino's script.

There was also Lawrence Tierney. Never exactly a great actor, more of a physical presence, really. I had completely forgotten about him, but he had this powerful physical force, and the fact that Tarantino thought of casting him suggested to me the film might be honest and true. These were actors you couldn't fake your way around. Quentin told me he would be thrilled to have the film shown at the Directors' Fortnight, but I told him I thought it deserved better—a spot in the Official Selection, and that's exactly where it ended up, out of competition. And then, two years later, he won the Palme d'Or with *Pulp Fiction*.

What makes Tarantino important in your eyes?

He's got incredible talent, a distinctive tone, and a world of his own that's in some way a visionary take on human nature. People often talk about his cinephilia, about all the references in his films, but that's not what gets me. His work goes far beyond being just a stylistic exercise. Every reference goes deeper than just a tribute to the filmmakers who influenced him. It opens up a very personal vision and serves the storytelling. *Jackie Brown* is my favourite of his films because it's probably the most personal, almost the least showy. That said, the second part of *Kill Bill* is also one of my favourites, even if I feel his whole body of work is consistent in quality. It's also true that he's a *passeur*, a transmitter of cinematic knowledge, helping younger generations rediscover older films. And for someone like me, who has spent a lifetime trying to share a passion for the films I love, it's heartening to think that young people who are into Quentin might, thanks to him, start taking an interest in older filmmakers they otherwise might have missed.

You still attend festivals and receive invitations worldwide.

Not as much as I would like. I still get invited, but because of my health, I can now only travel in business class, and not for reasons of comfort or vanity. It's medical. I can only go to places where friends might be able to point me toward good hospitals or surgeons if needed... But I still make it to Locarno, Cannes, Lyon, Mexico, Telluride, and I stay in touch with a lot of people.

Are you still seen as a scout?

I never thought of myself that way, even if, yes, I suppose I have done that, or at least helped. I just try to keep moving forward in life. And to do that, you have to see, feel, listen... People reach out a lot. I get sent scripts, people in Asia send me DVDs. I try to keep up as much as I can, but there's so much more coming out now than before—maybe too much—and much of it isn't important, which makes it harder to stay focused. Recently, I was really glad to be able to support the Argentine director Damián Szifrón and his film *Wild Tales* at Cannes and Telluride. He's a terrific talent I had spotted in Paris, and I don't think he's had the recognition he deserves. I like to think I helped audiences at Telluride take notice of him.

Of course, there have been disappointments too. *Life, Above All*, a South African film by Oliver Schmitz, never had the success it should have. I worked closely on fine-tuning it, and though it was included in Un Certain Regard at Cannes, I regret that it didn't make it into the main competition, where it might have gotten more attention. Roger Ebert and Richard Corliss—two major American critics, now gone—both wrote scathing pieces wondering why it wasn't included. Still, Sony Classics picked it up, and it was shortlisted among the nine foreign films for the

Oscars. I think a slot in competition at Cannes would have raised its profile and boosted its success, but it's a film I'm proud and happy to have supported.

It's true there are now too many festivals and too many different sections within the same festival, all fighting over the same films, which makes things trickier. And it's worth asking to what extent some of the people doing the selecting really have an eye for it.

I do feel frustrated sometimes that I can't champion certain films the way I once could. Back when I was discovering Asian filmmakers, I traveled alone—no office, no sales agent trying to sway me. I didn't have people pushing their agenda, trying to persuade me. And I think in that kind of position, you're more able to be clear-eyed, sharp, than when you're buried under a hundred DVDs or DCPs, with press kits and recommendations and all sorts of ways to spoon-feed your opinion.

Do you still read film criticism?

Not much. Back in the days of Mac-Mahon and those petty squabbles between cinephiles, we used to read a lot of it, but not anymore. These days, at least when it comes to French criticism, there's often this kind of bland consensus across newspapers, weeklies and magazines all year round, except during the Cannes Film Festival, when suddenly things flare up, tempers rise, and the name-calling begins again. That's when people start arguing left and right, calling certain screenings scandalous, even getting downright insulting toward a film or its director. I've always hoped someone would write a serious book on Rowland Brown or on wasted careers like Harry d'Abbadie d'Arrast, or other biographies, whether I knew the person or not.

Which are the most important festivals?

Cannes, of course, and when we talk about Cannes, we have to consider every section. Say what you will about it, but the festival is essential, and by itself it carries more weight than all the others put together. You can regret that certain films that should have been selected weren't, and that others were—even though, from where I sit, they didn't deserve to be. Take Cristián Jiménez's *Bonsái*, for instance, a Chilean film that struck me as pure intellectual masturbation, made by someone who doesn't know how to direct. You can also argue that the way the jury is composed doesn't always help ensure quality in the awards. Still, Cannes is unmissable, and remains the best shop window for a new film.

I'm nostalgic for the days when I could walk around with Robert Redford or Jack Nicholson without any security detail. We would talk about movies, stop at a café on the Croisette, and no one would bother us.

I haven't been to Venice or Berlin lately. I prefer festivals like Bologna, Telluride, Lyon or Singapore—more human in scale, where you can actually watch films in a way that feels geared toward real cinephiles, have conversations with audiences and filmmakers, and feel like part of a community, brought together by the shared pleasure that cinema fundamentally is.

THE MAN WITH THE CAMERA: PRODUCER AND DIRECTOR

How did you become a producer?

I started out as a film buff, and discovering new films gave me this gut-level hunger for other stories, ones I dreamed of seeing on screen. I remember being so taken with *Night and the City*, then coming across translations of then-unknown plays in the Théâtre National Populaire's journal, like *Woyzeck*. In my head, I could see Richard Widmark playing the lead.

When I finished military service in late February 1962, I needed to make a living, which meant that the idea of making short films drifted further away. I had this plan for a script called *Tuer un cheval* [*To Kill a Horse*] with Jean-Louis Trintignant, but I got swept up in other things. After Mac-Mahon Distribution had some success re-releasing older films, I started thinking about becoming a producer, in the creative sense of the word, which is a bit outdated now, but a bunch of the projects didn't pan out. One was a film called *Paris borgne* [*One-eyed Paris*], built around the three legendary one-eyed directors: Raoul Walsh, Fritz Lang and John Ford. They were all interested, but I should have realised they were already too old. The industry just wasn't in a place to take on something like that. I talked about it with Jean-Claude Michaud, a finance guy in television. Around that time, there was also talk of working with John Ford to adapt *Boule de Suif*, Maupassant's short story that inspired Ernest Haycox's *Stage to Lordsburg*, the source for *Stagecoach*. Unfortunately, Ford couldn't stop drinking on the flight to Paris and showed up in such bad shape we had to switch his hotel every day because nobody would keep him more than a night. There was no way I could introduce him to Michaud in that state, and the whole thing fell apart.

I tried to get two other projects off the ground based on books from the Série noire collection. The first was *A Very Private Island* by David Westheimer, writing as Z. Z. Smith. In a kind of romantic daze and thinking of Ida Lupino in *They Drive by Night* and James Cagney in *White Heat*, I imagined Raoul Walsh would direct. I got stuck on that idea, even though a lot of people were ready to finance the film—just not with Raoul Walsh. Other directors were interested, oddly enough, including Jacques Tourneur, who knew Westheimer, and Don Siegel, who wanted to do it with producer Walter Wanger.

In a different vein, I had earned Josef von Sternberg's trust after the re-release of *The Scarlet Empress*, which helped restore his standing in the eyes of many. But

Sternberg wanted complete carte blanche when it came to subject matter and budget, no limits.

Between your roles as press attaché, distributor, director and producer, how would you describe yourself?

My first idea was to move from screenwriting to directing, but life had other plans, and I got swept along—maybe too much so. I think I could have been an old-school producer. If I had been a bit slicker, more opportunistic, I probably could have done more and done it better. Everything in my life happened on impulse. It's hard to pin me down, except maybe the way Todd McCarthy put it in his documentary about me, in which he describes me as a "man of cinema." Over the years I have been called all sorts of things: scout, troublemaker, a brilliant press agent with a terrible temper. But I was never chasing a label. What mattered to me was the work and what it served. If that sounds pretentious, so be it, but I think what set me apart was my eye, which I believe has always been sharp. I doubt many people have had a career as scattered as mine.

Many of your production projects seem to have grown out of your encounters with filmmakers, often ones whose work you had released or re-released, like Abraham Polonsky.

Alfred Eibel and I took out an option on the Richard Matheson novel *Someone Is Bleeding*, which has long been admired in France, and I thought of asking Polonsky to direct. Abe and I talked a lot about how to adapt it; we were completely in sync, and things were moving ahead beautifully. Catherine Deneuve was interested, and because of that, Universal was ready to get on board through Jennings Lang. But then Hitchcock wanted Deneuve for one of his own projects. Universal ultimately didn't pursue it, but Deneuve wanted to stay available for Hitch, and that brought the Polonsky film to a halt. We also discussed projects with Cy Endfield, but his career was already winding down. And I tried—without success—to get a remarkable Edward Chodorov script produced, called *The Lynching of Elizabeth Taylor.*

Earlier, I had introduced Roger Vailland to Joseph Losey, who decided to adapt his novel *La Truite*. He held onto the idea for a long time. In 1964, during the last lunch I ever had with him, he asked me to work on it, but I backed out because I had doubts. I felt Losey had changed, and I had a hunch that the film—which was finally made in 1982—wouldn't be the one I had once imagined.

Then there was *Silver Street*, a screenplay Daniel Mainwaring told me about: a hard-edged story set in a city like
Chicago or Detroit, about a police inspector hunting a killer
in the world of prostitutes. The action revolved around a
bar, an apartment upstairs and a pool hall. Losey told
Mainwaring it would get made someday, but it wasn't for
him, and when Losey turned it down, I offered it to Jacques
Deray, who was very keen. Charles Bronson agreed to star,
but producer André Génovès, out of sheer laziness, didn't
want to leave Saint-Tropez that summer to come with us to
Spain, where Bronson was shooting, to lock things down.
This was when Bronson was at the peak of his fame after
Once Upon a Time in the West and *Rider on the Rain*.

*How do you explain that most of your production projects
never came to fruition?*

Perhaps they were often no more than vague ambitions.
I probably also lacked tenacity and the patience to wait
for decisions from people who were too slow, or from
too many potential partners who all had to come together.
I would move on too quickly, drop the whole thing, head
off to another city, tempted by a new idea.

One of the first projects could have been Fritz
Lang's final film, *And Tomorrow: Murder!* Lang had been
developing it in Germany with Conrad von Molo, the
producer who had edited some of his prewar films. Les
Films du Cyclope, working with Éditions de Paris, almost
co-produced it through Jean-Luc de Carbuccia, with whom
I would have liked to have worked, but the project collapsed
when Lang walked away, for a mix of complicated reasons.

Not long after, I experienced my first real disappointment. Sidney Buchman—the screenwriter of *Mr. Smith Goes
to Washington* and the man behind many of Columbia's
great comedies, from McCarey, La Cava, Cukor, Hawks—
was living in Cannes after being blacklisted. I used to see him
often, along with Edward Chodorov, another blacklisted
screenwriter, about whom Moss Hart writes about in his
autobiography. Sidney still had great cachet, and when Jay
Kanter left his post at Universal Europe, Arthur Abeles,
who was heading Universal, called Sidney to take over.
Sidney wanted me as his right-hand man. Everything was
falling into place, but then Sidney was diagnosed with an
aggressive cancer that quickly killed him.

I have always regretted not becoming an executive
like Sidney or Robert Lord at Warner Bros., Adrian Scott
at RKO, or Martin Racklin at Paramount. I think I could

have been very good at it. And when I finally had a chance to prove it—briefly, at Ciby 2000—I believe I did. The same kind of cancer also took Carl Foreman, just as he was preparing a film in China about Sun Yat-sen. He was planning to bring me onto that project too.

At the same time, in the 1970s, you had already begun working on a feature film script.

Not long before I made my short film *La Passe de trois*, I co-wrote a script with Alain Archambault called *Les Caprices de Sandy*. Alain had given me an unpublished manuscript I really liked, *Les Amitiés romaines*, which struck a chord with a story I had been thinking about, and I asked him if we could work on it together. Some scenes from that ended up forming the backstory of the character played years later by Feodor Atkine in my film *Cinq et la peau*. After my two shorts, Jacques Serguine came up with the idea for *Tuer un cheval*, which was somewhat in the same vein as Stanley Kubrick's *The Killing*, the story of a man hired to shoot a racehorse mid-race but can't bring himself to pull the trigger. I had shown Jean-Louis Trintignant my shorts and had him in mind for the lead of *Tuer un cheval*, which had almost no dialogue. The idea was to focus on this character as he gets ready to commit the crime. We would follow him in the street, in a café, with no clue what was going on in his head.

Were there other texts you wanted to adapt for the screen?

I once considered adapting Herman Melville's *The Lightning-Rod Man* and Heinrich von Kleist's *On the Marionette Theatre* into short films. Among ideas for features was also *Three Soldiers* by John Dos Passos, which I had imagined weaving together with Frédéric Prokosch's *Un chant d'amour* to create an epic about Americans before and after the war. I also thought about *Woyzeck* and, much later, Federico García Lorca's *Yerma*. The idea was to transpose it to the Philippines, with Gina Alajar and Phillip Salvador, shooting on video, the camera constantly moving among the actors, staying close, never cutting, right in the thick of things. That was around 1981–82.

As a producer, I also toyed with a film adaptation of Shakespeare's *King John*. That was shortly after seeing Leo McKern in Losey's *Time Without Pity*. He struck me as perfect for the role. I imagined Raoul Walsh directing it, not as a stately drama but as a galloping adventure.

Much later came another project: *The Dreamers* by Orson Welles, based on a story by Isak Dinesen. There were multiple versions of the script, all unfinished, all contradictory and riddled with brilliance and clutter in equal measure, and I thought I could see a way to make it work. In 1998, I sat down with Oja Kodar, Welles' last companion, and together we restructured the story, clarified the plot and sharpened the dialogue. It's one of the things I'm proudest of.

I also had an idea for something with Viviane Forrester, based on *Night Sky* by Chandler Brossard, about a young foreign girl who comes to Paris to have an abortion. In a church, she meets a man fighting cancer, and his will to live makes her want to keep the baby. It wouldn't have been an anti-abortion film. It was more a melodrama about a poetic connection between two people and their renewed embrace of life.

How did you come to make your first film, One Night Stand?

I went to Hong Kong in 1973. I was drawn to the idea of making a film there, mainly because of the city itself, which is so teeming with life that it makes you want to shoot something. I figured it would be cheaper too, and that I wouldn't have to go around begging for money. What drew me in was the idea of an outsider in a foreign city, in a completely different culture. The very end of Michel Déon's novel *La Corrida,* where a character finds himself alone, facing his future, and also the ending of Kenji Mizoguchi's film *Miss Oyu*, helped shape the concept of *One Night Stand*—or *Alibis*, as it's called in French—even though those influences faded into the background once the script took shape. Kenneth White and I worked hard on fine-tuning the dialogue.

You brought in White, a poet, to write the script. That was unusual at the time, and still is today.

Once we decided the main character in *One Night Stand* would be a translator of poetry, I thought: why not collaborate with a poet? I had just discovered Kenneth White in Pierre Leyris' French translation, and I thought he was the right person to write the dialogue. Getting poets involved in screenplays is something we still don't do enough of.

The film was plagued with difficulties, and only a few people ever saw it.

I made mistakes, no doubt. The shoot became very difficult, and that weighed heavily on the whole project. Bits of it still hold up. I think there are some interesting moments in the footage—fleeting glimpses of the city that are nicely captured—but the heart of the film just isn't there. Some of the blame lies with Richard Jordan. He was a brilliant actor, we were a disastrous match. Maurice Ronet had wanted to do the film, but since I wanted to shoot in English, I went with Jordan. Making the character a translator meant he was anchored in a cultural tradition that I understood, but when Jordan got on set, he tried to play the part as a charming ladies' man, when the character was supposed to be the opposite. What interested me was something that became central to my own life: someone alone in a foreign city. The film isn't autobiographical, but I could relate to what the character was going through.

We fought almost immediately. He couldn't accept that the audience should first see the character's darker edges and only later, through oblique turns, uncover something more human. But I felt it was more honest to begin by having the audience alienated from a character rather than to trying to win them over straight away. That disagreement created a constant conflict with Jordan, and it really hurt the film. I ended up having to shoot scenes that went against everything I believed in, ethically and aesthetically, so it was a bit of a surprise that, once it was edited, the film held together much more than I expected, perhaps thanks to certain visual and sonic textures that emerged along the way. The whole experience was crushing, and I think that's why it took me so long to even think about making another film.

One Night Stand was meant to be released in France in 1977, but the producer, André Génovès, went bankrupt and the film never came out. It was screened only for a few journalists, though the reviews were surprisingly kind. Jean-Louis Bory, in particular, was enthusiastic.

Is that what encouraged you to continue as a filmmaker?

Michel Piccoli happened to like *One Night Stand*, and we worked together on a script called *Transit*, about an airline pilot flying around Asia, drifting between cities and women, encountering different cultures. His job had become a kind of routine he was desperate to break out of. Piccoli thought that Jean-Claude Fleury, who I knew, and who later ran Ciby 2000, might finance it. but then Piccoli's production company went bankrupt.

A few years later, while I was working in the Philippines on re-editing some of Lino Brocka's films, I thought maybe I could shoot something again over there for very little money. Like Hong Kong, Manila just oozes cinema. Jean-Claude Fleury had always regretted that *Transit* didn't happen, but I wasn't patient; I needed things to move fast, so I wrote a screenplay where the dialogue was slightly off from the visuals, to avoid having to shoot with sync sound. And again, just on instinct, I thought of bringing in a poet—not so much to write the script from scratch, but to rework scenes and dialogue. This time it was Eugène Guillevic. We travelled through several Asian cities with his partner, Lucie Albertini, to give the characters more grounding.

Was this the project that led to Cinq et la peau?

Yes. I developed the idea for that film out of my experience—and the struggles—I had with *One Night Stand*. I thought: if I set it in Manila, with a foreigner as the main character, and avoid direct dialogue, then it could be made for next to nothing. I imagined a kind of kaleidoscopic film that would be part diary, part travelogue, part character study, part polemic, part poetic narrative—constantly shifting registers, linking sound and image not by strict continuity, but by the emotional resonance of the moment. Writing it was a fairly complex process. I worked with Alain Archambault, drawing on scenes from his two unpublished novels, *Les Amitiés romaines* and *Les Caprices de Sandy*, that in their own way were quite beautiful. We also pulled in repurposed sequences from *Transit* and stray verses by René Char, Montherlant and others. I borrowed a verse or two here and there, weaving them into the script in relation to the images. Fernando Pessoa's poetry had become central to me, and I think I managed to bring some of that dynamic into the script.

Cinq et la peau *was a great critical success, and it did well in arthouse cinemas. Were you eager to direct something else?*

I was definitely motivated to write another script—*Michelina*—but got swept up in working with Lino Brocka in the Philippines and, more broadly, into the whirlwind of the anti-Marcos revolution, so I wasn't able to really focus on the project until a few years later. The idea behind the script was simple: the relationship between a call girl and one of her clients. Answering machines, which people used all the time back then, played a big part, so the story is outdated now, at least in terms of technology. Even though the plot revolves heavily around the call girl's profession, the real action, where their relationship finds its truth, takes place elsewhere. The story was tied to how people lived at the time—planes, answering machines—and how those tools were used to seduce or humiliate. I still think it's one of the best things I've written. I wanted the story to unfold in a way that felt seamless, almost imperceptible, with a kind of quiet, constant humour that gradually revealed the heart of the film: a relationship that is shaped by the woman's profession but actually takes place on a deeper level. The only way to make the psychological dynamic between this kind of Stendhalian call girl and my protagonist work would have been to cast someone as magnetic as Alain Delon in the male role.

There would have been a lot of sex scenes, and I had a hard time settling on an actress. I was worried that they wouldn't be able to convey everything that was required. Casting became a huge problem, and I couldn't see how to solve it. If had to name one actress who might have come close, I would say Katharine Hepburn in some of her 1930s roles. The producer Jean-François Lepetit, fresh off the success of *Trois hommes et un couffin*, had set his mind on producing *Michelina* and even announced it in the press, but those casting issues delayed us and Lepetit got cold feet. After such a big hit, he was wary of taking a risk on something that might not do as well.

Did you think about directing something else instead?

I started thinking about a short story by Jean-Pierre Martinet, "Ceux qui n'en mènent pas large." Martinet had published a beautiful book in 1978 called *Jérôme*, set in a kind of Jim Thompson world—bleak, lyrical, deeply despairing, very much a reflection of who he was. We both had this same taste for darkness and cruelty. I had a feeling Yves Martin would be the perfect collaborator to work with Jean-Pierre. We ended up writing *Jacques Tourneur est mort* together, in a real spirit of complicity. We had a few actors in mind: Bernard Blier would have been ideal as the uncle, Guy Marchand would have nailed the part of the screenwriter who slyly eggs on the protagonist, and Richard Bohringer could have played the washed-up romantic lead perfectly.

That title, Jacques Tourneur est mort, *remained listed for years in the "projects" section of* Film français.

It was actually the opening chapter—self-contained and fully formed—of a novel that Jean-Pierre Martinet had decided never to publish. I developed a real fondness for him. He was wasting away working in television as an assistant director, but was a true cinephile, an old-school bachelor from the 1960s, obsessed with literature. He frequently came up to Paris from Tour, where he lived, so we could spend time with Yves Martin and sketch out the dialogue together, drawing on our regrets and memories as film lovers, and a gathering gloom about the direction society was moving in, an unease that time has only confirmed, and sharpened. I secured an advance on box office receipts, and if I had pushed harder and knocked on the necessary doors, the film could have been made on a modest budget. But this was also the period when I was helping Lino Brocka finish *Orapronobis*, a project that, in the end, turned out to be a big disappointment.

In 1992, you showed Jane Campion's The Piano *to Jean-Claude Fleury, then head of Ciby 2000, and began to position yourself as a producer. What kind of producer did you want to be?*

More of an executive producer, to be honest. I followed the films I worked on more like an old-school studio exec than a traditional producer. *The Piano* is probably the only foreign-language film funded out of France that went on to become a worldwide hit. I was deeply involved from start to finish—right from the script stage to the work print, on which I suggested a few tiny edits that I felt were minor but meaningful, then through all the preparations for Cannes. I hesitated for a long time before taking on a role like that. I was 55 at the time and starting to think seriously about my health, retirement, that kind of thing. In the end, my share of the success wasn't huge: $25,000 in salary and a $40,000 bonus. Between Ciby 2000 and later Pathé, I managed to carve out the possibility of a small pension.

Of all the stages in producing The Piano, *casting turned out to be especially tricky. Had Jane Campion considered other actors before Harvey Keitel and Holly Hunter?*

The first actor Jane thought of was Ed Harris. As for actresses, she was considering Sean Young, though we weren't exactly enthusiastic about that. Holly Hunter had heard through her agent that Jane was in Los Angeles casting. Since the lead character doesn't speak—though she does have occasional internal monologues—Holly managed to get her hands on the script and recorded an audition tape in which she wore no makeup and had her hair pulled back. She read the lines very simply, almost flatly. Jane called me up and said she had just received a remarkable tape and asked me what I thought of Holly Hunter for the role. I didn't know what to say because I was taken aback, mainly because of her accent, which I remembered from the Coen brothers' film *Raising Arizona*. But Jane was intrigued, met with Holly, and eventually cast her. Her agent was asking for a lot—a million dollars. But Sam Neill had already said he would do it for the same fee as everyone else, and I knew Harvey Keitel would be reasonable, so I arranged a dinner, and in the end we got everyone to agree to work for $250,000 each.

The success of The Piano *helped solidify your position and allowed you to get other projects off the ground at Ciby 2000 as executive producer.*

It opened doors. I was able to bring in Mike Leigh's *Secrets & Lies* and two films by Abbas Kiarostami, *Through the Olive Trees* and *A Taste of Cherry*. I had known Leigh since *Bleak Moments*, which Frédéric Mitterrand had distributed in France. It was thanks to *The Piano*'s success that I was able to secure a budget for *Secrets & Lies*, a budget that Mike had never had access to before.

I had also long admired Charles Burnett's films *Killer of Sheep* and *To Sleep with Anger*, and we got on really well while working on the script for *The Glass Shield*. Sadly, Charles wasn't assertive enough when dealing with his American producers, who weren't exactly powerhouses themselves, and when I pushed back against casting decisions I thought would ruin the film—even though Martin Bouygues had agreed to cover additional costs to hire stronger actors—they insisted on sticking with their original plan. The script was watered down, the characters lost their edge, and a number of scenes were either cut or altered beyond recognition.

After that, I went to see Robert Altman at his home in Malibu to ask what he wanted to make next and offer Ciby 2000's support. Right away he mentioned *Prêt-à-Porter*, a film he had been hoping to make for years. I wasn't too enthusiastic, so he brought up another idea: *Kansas City*, about Prohibition and jazz. He even said he could get Julia Roberts on board. He ended up making *Prêt-à-Porter* instead, and after that experience Julia Roberts didn't want to work with him again. I happened to be in Telluride while Altman was showing *Short Cuts* in Venice, so Ciby sent someone else to negotiate with his agent. The original budget was meant to be $5 million—Altman was good at working within tight budgets and getting actors to take pay cuts—but thanks to all the go-betweens, it ballooned to $20 million. I should also mention that I tried to bring *Pulp Fiction* to Ciby 2000, but that didn't work out either.

Ciby 2000 was a different kind of production company. What made it unique?

It was definitely one of a kind. The company was born out of industrialist Francis Bouygues' desire to get involved in filmmaking. He brought a lot of trust—almost a kind of faith—in what cinema could achieve. There was also, to be honest, a certain naïveté which sometimes led to paying inflated salaries and signing poorly negotiated deals.

What was your experience working with Pathé after leaving Ciby?

I was torn between Pathé and TF1, but I didn't want to be based in Boulogne, so I chose Pathé. It was close to the Champs-Élysées and I trusted François Ivernel. Later on, Jérôme Seydoux probably decided I wasn't "a money man." And the financial disaster of *Boesman and Lena*, certainly didn't help. It was a massive loss and pretty much pushed me to the margins. I began working in an executive role on Im Kwon-taek's *Chihwaseon*. I had initiated the project outside of Pathé, but eventually brought the company in. Unfortunately, a few directors I admired—Frankenheimer, Boorman, Schatzberg—ended up making things unnecessarily complicated in their own ways. For example, I had read a novel by Gustav Solin, a former assistant to Mauritz Stiller, about a lost film that Stiller and Garbo were rumoured to have shot in Turkey. I thought it was a beautiful piece of writing and mentioned it to Jerry Schatzberg. Solin agreed to let us adapt it. It was, in fact, practically already a script. But Jerry said he wanted Harold Pinter to write it. I asked if he realised what he was proposing: asking Pathé to put up $600,000 just to commission a script. That was the kind of thing that kept happening: friendships turning into artistic dead ends.

You worked with Jane Campion again on In the Cut *(2003), produced by Pathé. How did that reunion go?*

I got on extremely well with Jane while we were developing the script, but things started to go a bit sideways during casting. She had a few odd ideas, particularly when it came to the actors. She was absolutely set on Mickey Rourke, for example. Then, during the shoot, there were moments when she chose to film with a visual style that, to me, felt almost like an affront, like a slap in the face to everything I believed cinema should be. Some of the lenses and camera angles she went for were, at the very least, questionable, if not outright wrong. I was convinced she was making a mistake. I won't go into more detail, but it was quite painful and very intense. We've since made up, but it was a very rough patch.

THE ADVENTURER: JOURNEY TO ASIA

Was your departure for Asia part of a planned project, or more a matter of chance?

Chance, though my introduction to the continent had begun long before, first through Mizoguchi's films, then because of the Japanese texts, particularly Zeami's writings on Noh theatre,* that I was reading.

As I mentioned, I had also been strongly influenced by Henry Miller's writing. Then one day, Miller's agent, George Marton—a Hungarian based in Paris, who also represented Fritz Lang, Robert Siodmak and others—called me to say that Miller wanted me to see a Chinese film called *The Arch*, by Shu Shuen Tang. She was a Tang dynasty heiress living in exile in Los Angeles who had shot the film in Taiwan. Marton discreetly explained that Miller had fallen secretly— and platonically—in love with the film's star, Chinese actress Lisa Lu Yuan, who lived in Los Angeles, and he hoped I could do something to help the film. As it happened, I liked the film a lot and decided to release it in Paris. That was in 1969. It turned out to be a major critical success and, for the art-house circuit, a commercial one too.

I went to Hong Kong in 1973, at the request of Shu Shuen Tang, who was struggling to edit her second film, *Zaijian Zhongguo*. From that first trip, the real challenge was communication, getting across fine nuances with people who often didn't speak a word of French or English. I was completely without bearings and had to push the translators to clarify questions and answers, to really get to the heart of what was being said. I think I managed to communicate quickly in many situations, partly because I had already experienced building bridges with people much older than me, people like Lang, Walsh and Ford, whose backgrounds were utterly unlike mine.

I regret not going to Asia earlier. I might have discovered—or helped rediscover—certain filmmakers, which could have made a real difference to their careers, and sometimes even to entire national cinemas. When I think about the cinema of Hong Kong and Taiwan, which was essentially Mandarin-language at the time, I might have been able to bring *A Touch of Zen* to Cannes earlier, along with films by Li Han-hsiang and Sung Tsun-Shou.

Beyond Hong Kong, I'm thinking about Lino Brocka in the Philippines, Shin Sang-ok in Korea, and even earlier, as far back as 1964, Ritwik Ghatak, the Bengali filmmaker my Indian friends Sunil and Nargis Dutt told me about.

---

* *La Tradition secrète du nô*, translated by René Sieffert (Gallimard, 1960).

What was it about Asia that made such an impact?

The first thing that hits you is the atmosphere—the climate, the air, the humidity, the way it all feels on your skin. There's something in the air that gets under your skin before you even realise it. That's what happened to me in Hong Kong, later in Manila and elsewhere, despite the differences between each country. Then you're swept up in the sheer density of people, the teeming crowds, which are much livelier than anything you would encounter in France or America. There's also the food, which is a primary point of contact. Even the humblest restaurants are immediate entry points into the atmosphere, the smells, the flavours. Your senses wake up. From there, just as with films, you begin to feel new vibrations. It's through contact with people that you begin to engage with those sensations.

I also love going to local performances. I rarely go to the theatre anymore in France, but in each of these countries I have tried to attend something. That's less true for the Philippines, where Spanish influence has made the theatre more like our own, but in Japan, for instance, whether it's Noh or Kabuki—or even lesser-known forms like Bunraku—there's a whole range of sensory experiences at play. Across much of Asia, from India to Thailand, you come across versions of the *Ramayana*, the same story told by a narrator with musicians, and performed with puppets that vary from region to region. Sound plays a big part in all this too. Japanese music is fairly well known, but the sound of a Javanese gamelan orchestra, which often echoes the sounds of nature, is less familiar. It's something you have to hear at dusk, beneath a sky changing colour rapidly and dramatically. The sound of the kayagum, the Korean zither, can heighten your sense of nature. It's music that feels like torrents and forests. All these experiences tie in with the streets, the old cinemas, some of them practically ancient. It's like going from the chaos of a typhoon to a moment of calm air. You feel it in your whole body before your mind even starts to make sense of it. It's not unlike the feeling you get watching certain Raoul Walsh films, or some Westerns, or seeing New York streets during Prohibition in old gangster movies. There is something exhilarating and deeply physical about it. It's a way of getting out of yourself, of tapping into something primal, especially for those who don't have another outlet for catharsis in life.

I have often experienced that exhilaration in Asia, like a battery being constantly recharged. It's stimulation on every level: the streets, the art galleries, the big department stores where you could once find countless pieces of craftsmanship. The contact with calligraphy—in the streets, in books, in paintings—completely shifts your way of seeing and almost changes who you are. When I was burgled and a lot of my things were stolen, including books that had become a part of me, it really did feel like something had been amputated.

Did you see the continent as being in a state of transformation?

I was lucky enough to visit several countries just before they were swept up by globalisation. Hong Kong today is a far cry from what it was in 1973. The Manila of the Aquino and Ramos governments became very different from the Manila under Marcos. And Kuala Lumpur was still a provincial town when I arrived there in 1977. It has been completely transformed since. I remember meeting an Englishman there, David Shephard, a respected expert on Malay culture, who wanted to take me to a remote village in Borneo to witness the harvest festival, with all its ceremonies and performances. These days, in Indonesia, it's hard to come across *wayang kulit*—shadow puppetry—or *orang kulit*, where men wear elaborate masks and costumes, the way I saw them back then. Even in Japan, where Noh and Kabuki are officially preserved, only a privileged few now have the opportunity to see such things.

What was your first encounter with Asian cinema?

It came through Mizoguchi. On the day it opened at the Studio de l'Étoile, I saw *The Life of Oharu*, which came out a year before *Ugetsu*. Both films left a deep impression on me, though at the time I couldn't quite explain why. What struck me most was how close I felt to the characters, the flow of the storytelling and editing, and the restraint of the camera. It's strange to think of all the years that passed between my discovery of Mizoguchi and my encounter with *The Arch*. All that time I almost ignored Asian cinema altogether. I was so caught up in American films, and a few French or Italian ones, that pretty much shut myself off from other cinematic traditions—which, in fairness, were far less accessible back then.

You started in Hong Kong. Did you have any expectations there, in terms of cinema?

None at all. I knew about Bruce Lee, of course, but was completely unfamiliar with popular Hong Kong cinema.

I asked questions and watched films, some of which astonished me. The first one I saw in a cinema was Sung Tsun-Shou's *The Story of a Mother*, which is a remarkable melodrama. Then came King Hu's *The Fate of Lee Khan*, a film bursting with energy and invention, even though its final sequence—a long battle in the dunes—felt somewhat rushed compared to the earlier martial arts scenes, which were beautifully choreographed and shot. I was also struck by Li Han-hsiang's *Illicit Desire* and, to a lesser extent, by Kong Lung's *The Call Girls*.

I was captivated by Hong Kong itself, which felt almost like a fairytale. The city itself, the ferry crossing the bay, the food, the crowds, the warm rain that dries almost instantly on your skin... At the time, Hong Kong still felt like a provincial city. The full-on urbanisation came later.

It was a few months later, when you returned, that you discovered another King Hu film: A Touch of Zen.

I saw it in a heavily shortened version—about two hours and ten minutes—though the original ran three hours and five minutes. The film had flopped badly in both Hong Kong and Taiwan, and exhibitors had taken it upon themselves to cut it however they liked. By 1973, there were no complete prints left. No two versions were even alike. I was blown away by its visual splendour, the shot composition, the energy, the imagination behind it. I began working to acquire the rights, but King Hu, whom I trusted at the time, was on very bad terms with his producer, Sha Jung-Feng. He had essentially poisoned the well, and negotiating the rights required a lot of patience. Over a year later, we were finally able to start piecing the film back together and restoring the original five-minute opening credit sequence that Hu had scrapped out of fear it would alienate Hong Kong and Taiwan audiences. I thought it was magnificent. The restored version was re-released almost immediately in Taiwan and became the biggest box-office hit of all time there. Today it's a recognised classic not only in Taiwan and Hong Kong but abroad as well, and later even in mainland China. Of course, by then, no one in Taiwan remembered that back in 1973, the film had been hated by just about everyone.

At the risk of sounding heartless, Hu's death in 1997 left me completely unmoved. I think that has to do with two things: the huge personal disappointment he turned out to be, and the equally big letdown he became as a filmmaker after *A Touch of Zen*. He clung to every penny in a dishonest way, driven purely by ego, and let himself be manipulated like a puppet by his wife. After the Cannes success, he completely lost his grip. He never understood that *A Touch of Zen* had sprung from deep within—his culture, his instincts—and that it wasn't something he could repeat. *Raining in the Mountain* starts off quite well, but it never reaches the level of *A Touch of Zen*. During the period when I was close to him, we had many conversations about the script. The second half was already problematic, but Hu's laziness and carelessness toward the project meant he never really did enough work on it. That said, *Legend of the Mountain* isn't as bad as some have claimed. The story is silly, yes, but stylistically it's on par with *Raining in the Mountain*. I also tried to help him get a Western made in America. I introduced him to producer Mike Medavoy and his associate Marcia Nasatir, but he asked a fellow countryman to write the script, which was done quickly and badly, and that ended up sinking the whole project. From then on, he just kept declining, maybe because of the toxic relationship with his wife. He had started drinking heavily and his mind seemed to deteriorate.

This may sound harsh, but parts of my life that once mattered deeply—things I lived with passion and intensity—feel dead to me now. I know they happened, I know what they meant to me, and probably still mean something, but it's as if I lost an arm and it now lay beside me, no longer part of who I am.

Meanwhile, Hong Kong cinema was enjoying a bit of a resurgence, thanks to some theatrical releases in Paris. Were you aware of filmmakers like Chang Cheh and films like The New One-Armed Swordsman?

I don't recall Chang Cheh even being on anyone's radar at the time. His films were showing in Hong Kong, but I don't think critics paid them much attention. I probably didn't even know his name when I arrived in Hong Kong in 1973. As for Chu Yuan, I wasn't familiar with him either, though I did see *Intimate Confessions of a Chinese Courtesan*. Still, *A Touch of Zen* was the standout film. It overshadowed everything, and maybe that led all of us to overlook someone like Li Han-hsiang. But Hu's film was such a meteor. The irony is that *A Touch of Zen*, like Lino Brocka's *Insiang* in the Philippines, was considered a failure in its own country.

Perhaps if I hadn't already seen other unfairly dismissed films, like *Night and the City*, *Pursued*, *Puzzle of a Downfall Child* and *Leo the Last*, I might not have responded so strongly to the injustice done to *A Touch of Zen*.

When did your knowledge of Asia expand beyond Hong Kong?

In 1977, I travelled to Indonesia, Malaysia, Singapore, the Philippines and Korea, with a stop in Japan, which by then was fairly well explored. I decided to take a few months to get away, shake things up, move around, and discover new places. I had met an Indonesian poet named Taufik Ismail in Australia who told me to get in touch when I arrived in Indonesia and offered to help me discover local films and meet some filmmakers. I did see a few interesting works, though none that struck me as wildly important. From Jakarta I went to Singapore, only to discover that since independence from Malaysia, cinema had practically disappeared there. I continued on to Kuala Lumpur, where I met Jamil Sulong, a still somewhat active filmmaker, although no copies of his films were available. He had made quite a few films and gave me a sense of the history of Malaysian cinema. I also met John Nettleton—not to be confused with the English actor—who at the time was essentially the Minister of Culture. He mentioned Lino Brocka as someone I should look into in the Philippines. I had already heard of Ishmael Bernal back in Hong Kong from a critic named Mel Tobias. Those were the first names I brought up when I got to the Philippines. Brocka was filming in the provinces, so I didn't meet him on that first trip, but I did see *Insiang*, which, oddly, at the time was regarded as far inferior to his most famous films *Weighed But Found Wanting* and *Manila in the Claws of Light*. I was surprised at how little *Insiang* was appreciated by Filipinos themselves. I brought *Insiang* to Cannes, where it was extremely well received, and like *A Touch of Zen*, it's now considered—both in the Philippines and internationally—one of the country's greatest films.

During that first trip you met Ishmael Bernal.

He invited me to visit his set, and I saw firsthand how resourceful the team was. Despite working with outdated, bare-bones equipment, they made a full-length feature. None of his films were available in usable prints. That was already an issue back then, and sadly it's only gotten worse since in the Philippines and many other countries, where prints are in dreadful condition, incomplete, or the negatives have been lost altogether.

After discovering the Philippines and your enthusiasm for
Insiang, *you returned almost as often as you did to Hong*
Kong.

I developed strong friendships there, particularly with
Brocka and "Hammy" Agustin Soto, who really deserves
far more recognition than he has received. Brocka fascinated
me, not just as a filmmaker but also as a theatre director and
political activist. He had extraordinary energy and a terrific
sense of humour. Even when I wasn't in the Philippines,
I spent a lot of time focused on his work, getting his earlier
films shown at festivals, cinematheques and retrospectives,
then later helping him with new projects: *Jaguar*, *Bona*
and *Bayan Ko* [*This is My Country*]. I helped Lino secure
funds for prints and subtitling. With *Bayan Ko*, I put him
in contact with Vera Belmont, who fronted the money for
postproduction in Paris, which meant far better technical
quality. That way, I helped his films cross national borders.
Lino used to call me The French Connection, and that
nickname stuck. Imelda Marcos, the dictator's wife, was
furious about the success of *Insiang*, since it depicted the
Manila slums she would have preferred to hide. My name
alone was enough to make her bristle.

Brocka was deeply politically engaged. What was it like
being with him during the Marcos years?

His activism was tightly linked to the wider Filipino
movement rising up against the Marcos regime, and he often
took me along on protest marches. In 1985, I had just arrived
in Sydney when one of our friends, Tikoy Aguiluz, called
to tell me Lino had been arrested and jailed. The news was
met with complete silence. The hotel in Sydney was kind
enough to lend me their telex room, and I started calling
everywhere—to France, to the U.S. The first article about
Lino's arrest appeared in *Variety*, thanks to Todd McCarthy,
and then other outlets quickly followed. Protests came from
all over the world, and they played a key part in securing
Lino's release.

You were sometimes directly involved in editing Brocka's
films.

I first worked on an international version of *Jaguar* in 1979,
which was shorter and more focused. Even Lino admitted it
was better, though in truth it could have been refined even
further. He wasn't able to do more work on the edit because

the producer refused to spend any more money unless the film was selected for Cannes, and since it couldn't be exported, because the censorship board had blocked it, we never got to finish everything we had planned. Then, with *Bona* the following year, the collaboration flowed more freely. I had seen all the rushes, which were remarkable: intense, fast, fluid, full of energy. Lino shot one take per setup, with minimal waste. I suggested a few things, especially opening the film with the scene of the flagellants, which anchors Bona's character in the Catholic faith as it's still practised in the Philippines. Lino really liked that approach.

By the time *Bayan Ko* was underway, he asked me early on to come help, hoping to avoid the production issues he had run into on earlier films. I arrived three weeks into the shoot, before the editing had been started. The film was shot semi-clandestinely in extremely poor neighbourhoods, during strikes that were often broken up by the police, so we had to keep a low profile and be resourceful to get it done. Lino never set foot in the editing room. The film was shot almost in sequence, but the first week had been a disaster, and the early scenes dragged. I realised the film's opening was far too expositional, so I suggested an alternate structure that used a flashback. Lino and his screenwriter, Pete Lacaba, immediately embraced the idea and rewrote accordingly. Popular resistance to the regime was heating up. I was constantly switching hotels, and we kept changing editing rooms. There were more and more power cuts, which slowed us down. Through this film—which shone a light on the poor and the marginalised—Lino was trying to directly challenge the legitimacy of President Marcos. I eventually flew back to Paris with the material to finish the sound mix, and miraculously the film was ready for Cannes just 36 hours before the screening. It was later named Best Film of the Year by the British Film Institute. Sadly, this experience marked the swan song of my friendship with Lino. Years have passed since the disaster that was *Orapronobis*, but today the luminous friendship we shared for so long overshadows the painful experience and immense disappointment that production became. Lino was one of the most extraordinary people I have ever known.

How would you describe the relationship between Brocka and the Marcos government?

He was at one with the city of Manila and its people. He lived the life of the city in a way I've never seen anyone else do. That's where his fight against the Marcos regime began because he was like an urban Robin Hood who became more and more defiant. He was like a gadfly to Imelda Marcos, who couldn't stand what he did or said. He came to symbolise resistance to oppression. If the Marcos regime committed fewer atrocities than some others, the oppression was particularly vile because of the misery it created—the abuse and corruption.

After *Insiang* became a success, all eyes turned to Philippine cinema, and especially to Lino. Imelda Marcos gave the order that none of his films were to leave the country. It's thanks to James Bond that *Jaguar* made it to the Cannes Film Festival. I had met Sean Connery while he was shooting John Boorman's *Zardoz*. Lino, always looking for some celebrity backing, found out about this and immediately told me that Connery had once played golf in Marbella with none other than President Marcos. "If Connery asks for the film to be released," Lino said, "Marcos won't dare say no. He might even scold his wife to avoid tarnishing the country's image." So I got in touch with Boorman and sent a telex to Lino telling him the wheels were in motion. Lino took the telex straight to the head of censorship, Colonel Barbero, and even before we got Sean Connery to officially sign anything, the film was cleared for export.

I was in Australia in February 1986 when Marcos and his family fled the country. I don't think I've ever spent so much time in front of a TV screen. Since I had just wrapped up my work there preselecting films for Cannes, I was able to stop over in Manila and see the liberated city. Even on the plane, the flight attendants were celebrating Marcos' departure, and once on the ground, the euphoria with Lino and our friends made me momentarily forget the tensions between us. But Lino quickly became disillusioned with the new government. He had been thrilled at first that Tony Gonzalez, a Filipino producer, had been appointed Minister of Culture and Tourism, but Gonzalez immediately used the post to get his hands on the duty-free shops, and the signs of a new wave of corruption quickly appeared.

Was it disillusionment or weariness? Lino had changed. He didn't make any truly ambitious films between *Bayan Ko* and *Orapronobis*, and his commercial work during that period fell far below the standard of his best. He was slowly being seduced by fame, and a certain vanity crept in. He still talked, albeit less energetically, about making a film critical of the Aquino government, and in hindsight, I probably shouldn't have encouraged him. I had my doubts, and his energy was clearly fading. His cinematographer, Carding Baltazar, had died, but I saw *Orapronobis* as an excuse to spend another winter in Asia, and I already knew where I could get the funding. Still, the production was painful from the start. The crew wasn't nearly as good as before, the casting felt rushed, and Lino was clearly less in control of his direction. He also wanted the film to reach a broader audience, which made it heavily didactic. I kept fighting for the project, right up to the breaking point.

Some have suggested there were political motives behind Lino's death in a car accident, but my Filipino friends know the truth. Lino, who normally travelled in a small jeep that was expertly chauffeured, had recently bought a flashy car for his lover. That young man used to go out drinking at nightclubs, and the crash happened on a stretch of road where accidents are extremely rare—unless you're completely drunk. Lino had never worked as much as he did in those final years, and sometimes I wonder whether that accident wasn't a form of indirect suicide, the final gesture of someone who no longer believed in much at all.

Were there other filmmakers in Asia whose careers you helped launch but were cut short?

Shin Sang-ok, whom I met far too late, lived a life that was—at the very least—eventful. His story highlights one of the great tragedies of world cinema: the lack of curiosity shown by critics, festival directors and programmers toward Asian films. Most people were content with a vague awareness of Japanese cinema, and even that was limited to a handful of directors. Even Yasujiro Ozu, let alone Mikio Naruse, barely existed outside of Japan. And next door, in Korea, there was a compelling movement building. Shin Sang-ok was its most prominent figure, but there were also people like Yoo Hyun-mok, Kim Ki-young and Lee Man-hee. I was lucky enough to see films by Im Kwon-taek, who, though of the same generation as Shin Sang-ok, actually began his major work much later. Starting with *Mandala* in 1981, he built what is, to my mind, the most consistent and coherent body of work in all of Korean cinema.

The case of Shin Sang-ok is telling. His range was extraordinary, from intimate melodramas like *Mother and Her Lodger* to sweeping, almost Elizabethan historical epics like *Prince Yeonsan*, *Tyrant Yeonsan* and *Women of Yi-Dynasty*. I had first heard of him in the 1960s. Jacques Maréchal, of Grands Films Classiques, had seen one of his films at Berlin and wanted to acquire it, but he was never able to make contact. Shin's debut, *A Flower in Hell*, is remarkable. Despite its flaws—grainy stock, crude sound, rudimentary makeup, the full range of technical limitations you would expect from a Third World production of the 1950s—the film still hits with tremendous force. The camera is always in the thick of the action. It recalls the immediacy of early cinema while anticipating what would later be credited to the French New Wave. It really puts things into perspective. Often, we ascribe a sense of originality or power to a filmmaker from a particular country, when in fact similar qualities had already emerged—years earlier—in films made elsewhere.

If Shin's work had been recognised internationally, he might have been able to build on that momentum in South Korea, but the lack of global attention partly led the South Korean government to pass a decree shutting down his studio and barring him from filmmaking. He drifted around Asia for years, then disappeared entirely in 1978. He reappeared in Prague in 1983, on the set of a film being made for North Korea, at a time when many believed he had been assassinated by the South Korean CIA. Was he in North Korea voluntarily, as the regime claimed, or had he been kidnapped, as he would later insist? In 1986, he fled to the U.S. embassy in Vienna, and under American protection he took the risk of going to Hollywood, where he started a production company that had moderate success making commercial ninja films. All this despite not speaking a word of English. Before returning to South Korea during the democratic transition, he directed *Disappeared*, which includes some impressive crowd scenes. It's a scathing portrait of political corruption which, given the later indictment of two South Korean presidents, was eerily prescient.

The Indian filmmaker Ritwik Ghatak was likewise unable to realise a body of work worthy of his immense talent.

His films feel like fragments of a masterpiece shattered before it ever had the chance to exist. As early as 1952, he made *The Citizen*, which is an incredibly sensitive film—raw, vulnerable, ahead of its time. It took him years to get the chance to work again, and to this day it's baffling why films like *Ajantrik* [*Pathetic Fallacy*, aka *The Mechanical Man*] and *The Cloud-Capped Star* were never recognised in Europe. There are suggestions that Satyajit Ray, who was known to be extremely proud and arrogant, wanted to keep his status as the sole celebrated Indian filmmaker in Europe, and may have sabotaged efforts to promote Ghatak. During a visit to India, Georges Sadoul reportedly saw *Ajantrik* and recommended it to Favre Le Bret for Cannes. Favre Le Bret didn't have Ghatak's contact details, so he sent a telex to Ray, asking him to help establish contact. There was never any reply, and Le Bret dropped the matter.

Ghatak was a fragile man who was quite young when he fell into alcoholism. At least three of his films were left unfinished. He taught at the film school in Pune, made a few shorts, and eventually managed to complete a beautiful film in Bangladesh, *A River Called Titas*, which exists in two versions—one clearly superior to the other. That was followed by a rather pitiful final film, *Reason, Argument and a Story*, financed by the Indian government shortly before his death. It has been shown in retrospectives, but it should really be treated as a clinical document, a portrait of someone ravaged by alcoholism whose mind was no longer functioning as it once had. He plays himself in the film and comes across as lost, a shadow of the intellect that shines through his greatest work.

When I first met Nargis Dutt and her husband Sunil in Cannes in 1964, they spoke of Ghatak with awe, calling him a far more "Indian" filmmaker than Ray. After discovering his work, I came to agree. In fact, I now find it difficult to watch Ray's films with a completely clear conscience.

Were there other filmmakers who impressed you in India and Sri Lanka?

Mehboob Khan, in India. Large parts of his films are unbearable, but then, out of nowhere, come long stretches of brilliance. Pure cinematic splendour, carried by a kind of exceptional lyricism. This is especially true in his most beautiful film, *Humayun*, made in 1945. The characters begin a scene in a fairly conventional way, then, little by little, as the emotional intensity rises, the spoken dialogue explodes into song and music, expressing heartbreak and ecstasy with sublime intensity.

In Sri Lanka, I was taken with the work of Lester James Peries and his wife Sumitra, also a filmmaker. Lester is a truly great director, now very old, and far too often overlooked. His masterpiece, *Gamperaliya*, is a kind of Chekhovian story that spans several years in the life of a small community. Beneath the social and generational upheavals lies a quiet devastation, a terrible gentleness, a nostalgia for the past, a mix of resignation and protest in the face of life's harshness. Lester in effect invented Sri Lankan cinema with *Rekava* in 1956, a film that went unnoticed when it screened at Cannes. It's hard to understand how *Gamperaliya* wasn't recognised much earlier. Many years later, in 2002, he made another truly beautiful film, *The Mansion.*

In Malaysia, you got to know a filmmaker who became very dear to you: U-Wei Haji Saari.

During my second visit to Malaysia, I saw two of his television films, made shortly after his return from America. They already showed promise. A few years later, he directed his first feature, *Perempuan, Isteri dan Jalang* in 1993. It's uneven but is interspersed with moments of real brilliance. He also told me about a little television film he had made called *The Arsonist*, adapted from Faulkner's short story "Barn Burning." As with King Hu and Lino Brocka, I made several trips and raised the money to help turn it into a proper theatrical feature, with support from Pierre Mallet, the cultural attaché. The funding from the French government prompted the Malaysian government to chip in a little as well. The film screened at Cannes and was widely considered one of the best in the Un Certain Regard section. At the Telluride Festival, three very different people—Zhang Yimou, Werner Herzog and Bertrand Tavernier—all told me they liked it, which says a lot about the film's deep humanity. Vincent Sherman, who had known Faulkner personally, thought it was the best adaptation of the writer's work. And yet not a single cent was offered in Malaysia to support U-Wei after that critically and culturally significant success.

Finally, among the filmmakers you helped bring to wider recognition is Abbas Kiarostami.

What began as admiration for his early films gradually deepened into trust, and eventually into a quiet camaraderie. Over the course of several encounters, we discovered we were on the same wavelength, whether talking or traveling together, as we did during the making of *Through the Olive Trees* and *A Taste of Cherry.* I remember one particular trip we took to the Korean countryside where we spoke only of trivial things: the landscape, the feel of air on the rocks, the shades of green in the forests. Yet in those seemingly idle moments, I came to understand something essential about Kiarostami's relationship to space—both expansive and exacting—as one of the defining traits of his films, along with his profound clarity of vision.

Abbas never ceased to surprise me. In *Certified Copy*, there was already something quietly subversive, a discreet, unsettling indecency beneath the film's formal elegance. But even after having spent so many years with him, nothing prepared me for *Like Someone in Love*, the film he made in Japan. It moves almost imperceptibly, slipping past the defences of its characters, and its audience, to touch upon something raw and hidden. It probes the most intimate feelings, often still unknown even to those experiencing them, and captures with unerring precision the quiet mechanisms of fate, which draws people together only to cast them apart again, exposed and fragile. The deeper that sense of dread and clarity becomes while watching *Like Someone in Love*, the more mysterious and opaque the film seems to become. In its mise en scène—an art now almost forgotten, buried under hollow aesthetic prejudices—the film recalls Preminger at his height. But Kiarostami's aim isn't to show off. The film simply *is*: concrete, physical, enigmatic to the brink of revelation. You come away knowing something more about life.

After so many misunderstandings in my relationships with others, it was with Abbas that I think I truly learned how to better anticipate and navigate conflicts or misunderstandings—things I hadn't managed in my younger years, when I would clash too easily and get hurt too quickly.

Since Kiarostami's international breakthrough in the 1990s, people have often spoken of "Asian cinema" as if it were a single, unified entity. How did you view this trend?

Even Chinese cinema alone is made up of many Chinas, many generations. In Hong Kong and Taiwan, directors like Li Han-hsiang and King Hu created a kind of Mandarin cinema-in-exile that carried forward traditional Chinese forms, but the next generation—emerging at the end of the 1970s, with Ann Hui, Allen Fong Yuk-ping and Tsui Hark, a Vietnamese immigrant in Hong Kong—was light-years away from that classical cinema. In the early 1980s, filmmakers from Taiwan's New Wave—like Hou Hsiao-hsien and Edward Yang—initially felt quite distant from the Hong Kong scene, and in Edward Yang's case, closer to the West. He died too soon, leaving behind a body of work that, I believe, was still evolving. He and I used to talk at length about more ambitious future projects.

Fred Tan, of the same generation, was steeped in the influence of Li Han-hsiang. His *Rouge of the North* is a quietly beautiful adaptation of a novel by Eileen Chang [Zhang Ailing], the great Chinese writer who made her home in Hong Kong. Meanwhile, in mainland China, the emergence of Chen Kaige marked the beginning of the so-called Fifth Generation. These filmmakers, many from the Xi'an studios under Wu Tianming's guidance, stepped into the void left by the Cultural Revolution. The films of Xie Jin—*Two Stage Sisters*, just before the Revolution, and *Legend of Tianyun Mountain*, just after—belonged to an earlier, more traditional form, but starting with Zhang Junzhao's *One and Eight* and Chen Kaige's *Yellow Earth*, both shot by Zhang Yimou, there was a striking renewal in mainland Chinese cinema. It marked the arrival of a new kind of modernity, distinct from what was happening in Taiwan.

Of course, every Asian country has its differences, especially in terms of rhythm. Thai cinema of the 1970s, for example, with roots in oral storytelling traditions, often embraced a slow, repetitive tempo, whereby stories could be retold, meandered through, and revisited at will. I also think of Indonesia and the *dalang*, the puppeteer in *wayang* performances who lends his voice to all the characters and narrates the story. That figure echoes through the work of Garin Nugroho, where scenes unfold as if spoken or sung, often accompanied by music.

And then there is Hou Hsiao-hsien. His work now stands as one of the great achievements of the past forty years, and I don't believe it has reached its end. What a journey it's been since *The Sandwich Man*.

THE MONSTERS: MEMORABLE ENCOUNTERS

Fritz Lang is the filmmaker who comes up most often in conversations. There seemed to be a sense of kinship between the two of you. Under what circumstances did you meet him?

Along with Michel Mourlet and Michel Fabre, I met Lang in 1959. He was accompanied by Lotte Eisner during a retrospective of his work at the Cinémathèque on Rue d'Ulm. We spoke with him for more than an hour about the films we already knew and listened as he discussed those we hadn't yet seen. He seemed intrigued by our curiosity. Since his visit had been arranged by the distributor of *The Tiger of Eschnapur* and *The Indian Tomb*, Lang asked us which of the two we preferred. The films hadn't been warmly received, and most people leaned toward *The Indian Tomb*. We hesitated. I finally took the plunge and said, timidly, *The Tiger of Eschnapur.* Lang immediately replied, in French, "Moi aussi. C'est une masse de fonte !" ["Me too. It's a hunk of cast iron!"]

Later, at Claude Makovski's home, I saw the French version of *Hangmen Also Die!* on television. I liked the film and was intrigued both by what I sensed of Brecht's contribution and Hanns Eisler's music. Two German actors particularly stood out: Alexander Granach—who is in Arthur Robison's *Warning Shadows* and Murnau's *Nosferatu*—was extraordinary as the inspector, acting with a physical impulsiveness and urgency that are all too rare. Another actor, Reinhold Schünzel, acted with tremendous subtlety, bringing a sense of comedy and detail that gave real depth to his character.

Claude and I decided to re-release *Hangmen Also Die!* He had just founded a small production company but didn't have the money to buy the rights. My father stepped in and loaned us the money—bravely, for someone of modest means—and Claude covered the distribution costs. The film opened at the Pagode cinema, and although it wasn't an immediate success, my father eventually got his money back. I really have to salute him for taking that risk. It wasn't a huge sum, but it was still a gamble, and the film's slow start only added to the anxiety.

The image people have of Lang is still largely shaped by how Godard portrays him in Contempt.

Yes, but the dialogue Godard puts in Lang's mouth feels far removed from anything Lang himself would have actually said, even if his physical presence and natural gravitas are very much there. Lang was volatile, quick-tempered and could flare up at the slightest provocation. He could be acerbic, even cruel, with some people, but could just as easily be very tender. There were times when he spoke with deep nostalgia for prewar Paris, especially when we dined at certain restaurants that stirred his memories. He once admitted he was still in love with Gerda Maurus, whom he had met while filming *Spies*, decades earlier. Above all, when he spoke of the people he had loved, he always began with his mother.

At times, though, he would erupt like a wounded animal lashing out, and you had to find a way to soothe him. He wasn't the intellectual thinker many critics imagined. Lang could never have dissected his own work with the kind of academic rigour that others later brought to it. He was far too fiery, always reacting in the moment.

He insisted on airtight logic in his screenplays. While preparing *And Tomorrow: Murder!*, his final serious project, he consulted psychoanalysts at length. "They told me I am CORRECT!" he said, emphasising the word. But then on set, working out the action and the actors' blocking, he proceeded almost entirely on intuition. In *The Big Heat*, when Lee Marvin throws a cup of scalding coffee in Gloria Grahame's face, the way Lang set up and shot that moment made it feel like a pure impulse, one that he had fully internalised.

This idea of space seems fundamental in Lang's films. I recently rewatched *The Testament of Dr. Mabuse* on TCM and was immediately struck by the aspect ratio—1.17 or maybe 1.20, whereas I had only ever seen it projected in cinemas at 1.37. Years ago, I saw Ophüls' *The Bartered Bride* in that same format, which was used for a handful of films at the time. I'm convinced that every shot in *Dr. Mabuse* was composed for that format. That's no trivial matter, because it completely alters our perception of the film. Something so minor, you might ask. Well, yes. Even a small change like that makes a big difference because every shot feels completely locked in, tightly constrained by the frame and the space around it.

I remember leafing through a booklet published by MoMA on Lang. He had personally added notes for each film, and to my surprise, *Human Desire* was listed as 1.66, though I had only ever seen it in 1.37. At the time, projection equipment varied from country to country, city to city, even cinema to cinema. Unless a film was shot in CinemaScope, it might be screened in 1.33, 1.6 or 1.85, even SuperScope or RKO-Scope. Allan Dwan, who made films in the silent era, once told me that his 1955 film *Tennessee's Partner* was ruined by being shown in RKO-Scope or SuperScope. Just days after re-watched *Dr. Mabuse*, I saw *M*, again on TCM, and again in that same earlier format. The same conclusion holds: this tighter format is crucial to the film's power. If 1.66 feels more assertive and appropriate for *Beyond a Reasonable Doubt*, it's far less convincing for *While the City Sleeps*, which might feel sharper and more precise in 1.33. If you watching Don Siegel's *Invasion of the Body Snatchers* on TCM, you can see that it plays far better in 1.66, which really opens the film up.

There's something novelistic—almost gothic—about Lang's life story.

For many years, he never spoke of his first wife. And whether in Paris or elsewhere, I always saw him keeping to his agenda with extraordinary precision. Failing to jot down the exact time of an event would plunge him into a state of anxious restlessness, relieved only when I could confirm the missing detail.

"Pierre, at what time did so-and-so arrive? What time did I get that call?"

"Around eight, maybe eight-thirty…"

"I'm not asking *about* what time. I need to know: what time EXACTLY?"

One day I asked him why those few minutes mattered so much. His reply was unequivocal: "If you had ever been suspected of murder, you would understand."

Did he, as some later claimed, invent that whole story about being suspected in the death of his first wife, just as he invented other things? Maybe. But I'll never forget the emotion in his voice. And what I heard, in that moment, was the voice—terrifying in its sincerity—of someone who had nearly been wrongfully found guilty.

Were there other gaps in Lang's biography that you wish you had explored with him?

I do regret not pushing him further about his Paris years, between 1911 and 1914. And I also wish I had challenged him more directly about his travels. I was already fairly convinced he never went as far as Indonesia, and maybe not even Egypt. He never once mentioned any specific anecdotes about those places in our conversations. Just as his early films were drawn to exoticism, I suspect he thought it would seem more romantic or adventurous to claim in his biography that he had wandered that far afield.

At the time, directors were seen as infallible, the ultimate authority. If they said something, it wasn't considered a lie. Their memory couldn't be wrong. But now we know how often that just wasn't true. Had we questioned these things back then, we might have matured a little faster. You can view *The Tiger of Eschnapur* as just an exotic comic book, but there's no doubt in my mind that Lang used it to express his own fears and his sense of wonder. That it tells us more about him than it does about India is beyond question.

When he spoke about *And Tomorrow: Murder!*, it felt as though you were watching the film come to life before your eyes. I remember, in one of our first conversations, he talked to me about *House by the River*, a strange, then little-known film I hadn't seen. He described the beginning in vivid detail, with extraordinary visual recall and emotional force, as if it were something he had just experienced. When I finally saw the film, the impression I had watching it was remarkably close to what I had felt when listening to Lang describe it.

He also nearly made another film in India around 1961 called *The Mystery of the Black Jungle*, which was eventually directed by Mario Camerini. I never read the script, but I did read a long, very dense synopsis, full of plot twists and surges of barely concealed fury. It felt unmistakably Langian. He later gave me a version of *Man Without a Country*, a screenplay he had developed with Jonathan Latimer as early as 1940. Much of what you find in his anti-Nazi films—especially the *Mabuse* ones—was already there. Elements of that project later found their way into *Fly by Night*, which was directed by Robert Siodmak.

Until 1967, I still hoped Lang might make another film. He was approached again in the early 1970s by André Génovès, but by then I had little faith. Lang scribbled one or two pages of notes, then stalled. Michel Piccoli was meant to be involved and he was wonderfully supportive, but the post-1968 climate gave Lang ideas that were, in truth, a little naive. He wanted to set the story in the world of student protest, of young people rising up against the establishment. The only scene he actually came up with was of a student, tripping on acid, falling from a window and impaling himself on a fence.

Fritz Lang's personal life was clearly very complicated.

Yes, both the years leading up to his divorce from Thea von Harbou and his relationship with Lily Latte, his official companion, not to mention several other women. Latte, whom Lang eventually married so she could receive his pension after his death, was actually a hugely stabilising presence for him during their time together. After his death, she took it upon herself to protect his legacy, destroying the diaries he had kept obsessively for decades so no one would discover he had frequented call girls or had ongoing affairs. Those notebooks would have offered incredible insight—details about his aborted projects, the periods when he feared he might be blacklisted, and other murky areas of his life. The more you get to know Lang in practical, down-to-earth terms, the more you become aware of the darker, more hidden side of his work.

One particularly murky episode concerns his departure from Berlin in 1933, which was almost certainly more premeditated than he claimed.

One of my biggest regrets is not having had a tape recorder the day I spoke to Dan Seymour, an actor and close friend of Lang's who appeared in several of his films. He gave me a completely different version of Lang's escape from Germany, worthy of a scene from one of Lang's own thrillers, in which he left a car abandoned on the German side of the border. "But he left by train!" I protested. Seymour insisted otherwise: Lang was in the car, while his valet was on the train, wearing an identical trench coat and hat. Lang had deliberately made a public show of being out drinking in Berlin's trendy bars with a woman, pretending to get drunk while secretly dumping his drinks on the floor. He drove her out to the suburbs to make it seem like they were having an affair, just in case anyone was watching. Once he was convinced that no one was following him, he set off for the border. At the final stop before France, he got on the train as his valet got off to drive the car back to Berlin. Dan Seymour claimed to have heard that version before Lang started repeating the one that proved so effective in interviews and retrospectives, the story in which he escapes by train after Goebbels offers him control of German cinema. The now-famous tale of his meeting with Goebbels—where Lang supposedly says, "But my mother was Jewish," and Goebbels replies, "We decide who's Jewish"—had become what you might call a fictional truth, yet Lang always swore up and down that he never lied because, as he said, "To lie, you have to be sure you can remember your lies."

Another complicated chapter was Lang's navigation of the McCarthy era.

Lang had convinced himself he was on the so-called gray list, but of course, no such list ever officially existed. The term referred to people who were thought to be on the verge of being blacklisted. Take Daniel Mainwaring, for instance, who used his pen name, Geoffrey Homes, to front scripts written by others. His friendships with people like Joseph Losey, Paul Jarrico, Waldo Salt and others made him look suspicious, so he started signing his real name again to show he had nothing to hide. Lang, for his part, had helped the composer Hanns Eisler—who was later accused of being a Soviet spy—and Bertolt Brecht when they arrived in California in the late 1930s. He had also signed several petitions. In the climate of the time, all that might have made him feel exposed. But later, as his career was winding down, the idea of this unofficial gray list gave him a kind of explanation, a reason why the phone wasn't ringing, why work had dried up. It was easier to believe that he had been informally blackballed than to face a broader loss of interest in his work. He remained close with several blacklisted figures: Howard Dimsdale, Albert Maltz, Ring Lardner Jr. and Silvia Richards, who had also been his lover.

What were Lang's favourite films among those he directed?

I remember the flush that came over his face when a critic brought up *Moonfleet*, a film still beloved by many, but not one Lang thought highly of. His expression in that moment said it all: *Not this nonsense again!* Among his American films, his favorites were *Fury*, *Hangmen Also Die!*, *Scarlet Street*, *The Big Heat* and *While the City Sleeps*. Of his German films, his clear favourite was *M*. He resisted being dubbed the "author" of *Metropolis*, likely because of Thea von Harbou—his ex-wife—who had written both the novel and the screenplay. Still, it's impossible to imagine he wasn't deeply involved. I remember hearing him once shout, in his thick accent: "I am not a German! I am an American! An American!" He saw very few people in his final years. Ray Bradbury would visit him, along with Dan Seymour and Peter Lorre's widow. Like Walsh and Ford, Lang suffered from the absence of real film projects. None of them retired willingly; they were pushed aside.

Under what circumstances did you meet Raoul Walsh?

The first time I had direct contact with him was in 1963, when I was trying to persuade him to come to Paris for the re-release of *Objective, Burma!* We had barely begun speaking on the phone when he said, "Pierre, hold on a second…" One second passed, then two, then three. He came back to the phone and said, "I've got to hang up. Someone just shot John Kennedy." He was watching television. I turned on the radio, and a minute later the news came through. I've often wondered whether, because of that call, I was the first Frenchman to hear the news, and from the man who many years earlier had played Lincoln's assassin in *The Birth of a Nation*.

Walsh carried the weight of a life fully lived — and fully imagined. He had a vivid inner world. I once mentioned this to him and he replied, "My father was Irish, my mother was a Spanish gypsy. It's a mix of blood that gives you imagination."

He had a marvellous sense of humour and a storyteller's instinct that brought his anecdotes to life. He was modest too; I never once heard him boast. Like Hawks or Lang, if one of his films didn't succeed, he simply assumed it wasn't any good. When I ran through a list of titles for a retrospective to accompany the premiere of *Objective, Burma!*, he kept saying, "Pass it up, pass it up…" — even about a film I find magnificent, like *Pursued*, which was a major flop at the time. When we finally met in person, he told me two things that say it all. I asked him which of his films was his favourite. He named *The Strawberry Blonde*, a film I hadn't seen at the time. It had been a big hit when it was released, but it's not the first title people associate with Walsh today. But he had a deep personal connection to it — its story, its mood and its atmosphere were steeped in memories of his youth. That affection gives us a real clue to understanding other films of his, like *The Man I Love*, which he didn't like, simply because it hadn't found an audience. When you think of *The Strawberry Blonde*, you really feel that this is someone born in 1887 — someone who, as a child, witnessed the close of the nineteenth century and the dawn of the twentieth. The film is infused with nostalgia for that time, and for everyday heroes like the one played by James Cagney. In spirit, it feels very close to *Gentleman Jim*.

What is your most vivid memory of Walsh?

When he told me that "every shot must carry the film's centre of gravity." That, in an indirect way, echoes what he once said to *Variety* — and which was quoted in *Présence du cinéma* — about how there is only one single correct place to put the camera in order to capture the action. Few filmmakers have that kind of instinctive, unpretentious clarity. His films were made in the heat of the moment, with action as their backbone, and the direction stemmed from that.

Walsh's wanted Ida Lupino for *They Drive by Night* at a time when she had only played relatively minor roles. Walsh had previously worked with her on *Artists and Models*, in which she played a very small part, and when he suggested her for *They Drive by Night*, Jack Warner was surprised but agreed to a screen test, which Walsh insisted on doing with George Raft, who was already cast in the lead role. Walsh said he would do only one take, no rehearsals, and that take would be used in the film. Lupino confirmed this to me. It's exactly what happened. She was given no specific direction; they just talked casually about this and that. Then, as he rolled a cigarette, Walsh asked her, "Ida, you feel ready? Let's go." That take is in the film. Given all that's been said about directing actors, what's interesting about this anecdote is that Walsh's accumulated life experience allowed him to sense that Lupino was right for the role.

What do you think of Lupino's films as a director?

I always admired her as an actress, especially in Jean Negulesco's *Road House*. When I discovered she had also directed films, I was curious to see them. That curiosity became a revelation—shared with Michel Mourlet and Michel Fabre—when, in London, we came across *Not Wanted*, which was credited to Elmer Clifton. The film overwhelmed us with its urgency, immediacy, its stripped-down honesty, and its instinctive cinematic intelligence. Though Lupino wasn't credited as director, rumours had long circulated that she had directed most of it. That was later confirmed to me by actress Sally Forrest, actor Leo Penn, cinematographer Henry Freulich, and one of the screenwriters, Malvin Wald.

I met her for the first time in 1965 or 1966, during a trip to California. Collier Young, the producer, screenwriter and her ex-husband, worked next to Don Siegel's office. I asked if they were still on good terms. He said yes, and when I asked whether a meeting might be possible, he assured me it could be easily arranged. The next day, I met her. It was an incredibly awkward encounter. When I arrived, she was already seated at the bar. I began to speak but quickly stumbled over my words and sensed she didn't fully understand me. Was it my accent, or had she been drinking? At one point, she asked me to shift seats and speak into her other ear. That's when I learned that, at the age of 15, she had contracted polio, which left her partially deaf in one ear, a biographical detail reflected in *Never Fear*, her second film, which I later released in France. When we eventually sat down at a restaurant, she apologised for drinking, explaining that she didn't know how to respond to me. It's likely my questions were too eager, too cinephilic in tone. She told me again that she had drunk too much because she was overwhelmed—touched, even—that a young French intellectual had sought her out and admired her films.

Her work had largely gone unnoticed by American critics, but across the films there is a remarkable continuity, and they have by now been rediscovered and rightly recognised for their worth. The recent restorations of *The Hitch-Hiker* and *The Bigamist* show what a woman of character she was, and what a bold director. She operated outside the studio system to make films with a social edge, sometimes disturbing ones, like *Never Fear*, about a woman with polio, and *Not Wanted*, about the fate of unmarried mothers cast out by puritanical America. There's no melodrama in her treatment of serious issues, just a clarity of direction and a restraint in performance that feel strikingly modern. Sadly, she wasn't a savvy businesswoman. *Not Wanted* was a success, but the films that followed were not. She made them too quickly. She should have made fewer films, preparing and promoting them with greater care. Had her films been made just a few years later, they might have found a completely different reception. Cassavetes came along soon afterward, at a more favourable moment to establish a similar kind of career. There are points of contact between Lupino and Cassavetes, at least in their marginal position outside the Hollywood mainstream. Cassavetes, though he struggled, was able to build a body of work that Lupino couldn't, simply because the times didn't allow it.

Ford seems to have left less of an impression on you than other "dinosaurs."

Not at all. I met Ford when no one was offering him work anymore. He was a Machiavellian figure, and he played the part. He could steer people exactly where he wanted with lightning speed. Was it shyness that made him dodge questions and avoid opening up? He always managed, with a child's cunning, to throw people off balance. And he had a tremendous sense of humour. Like Walsh, he rooted his wild imagination in Ireland. He could be extremely cutting with some people, but I was never on the receiving end of that. Whenever I came to Los Angeles, I was immediately invited to his home.

Did you ever manage to bring together filmmakers you knew individually?

Yes, though often with disappointing results. At Carl Theodor Dreyer's request, for instance, a dinner was arranged with Henri-Georges Clouzot, Robert Bresson and Jacques Tati. You might expect sparks from such a gathering, but it was strangely inert, like a blank page on which nothing was written. Clouzot was charming, Tati taciturn, Bresson insufferably vain, and Dreyer painfully shy.

Another example was in 1967, when Fritz Lang, Jean Renoir and John Ford were all attending the Montreal Film Festival. I asked whether they might like to meet. They all agreed, on the strict condition that none of them would have to take the initiative. Back in 1940, all three had been working at Fox at the same time: Renoir was directing *Swamp Water*, Ford was filming *How Green Was My Valley*, and Lang was working on either *Western Union* or *Man Hunt*—I can't recall which. I don't remember exactly how I managed to coordinate it, but eventually they all met, briefly, at the entrance of the Queen Elizabeth Hotel. The meeting lasted about an hour. It was cordial, but never rose above small talk.

The last such episode I recall was with Fritz Lang on the day Luis Buñuel was to receive the Légion d'honneur at Jean Renoir's home. Buñuel had specifically asked that Lang be there; he had once said that seeing *Destiny* had awakened his desire to become a filmmaker. Lang was flattered and delighted, and we went together to the gathering. Buñuel made his declaration and Lang feigned surprise, as though he hadn't known in advance. Apart from that brief flicker of emotion, nothing more passed between them.

When did you meet Jim Thompson?

In 1965. At the time, only four or five of his novels had been translated in the Série noire collection, and just two or three of them truly stood out. What fascinated me most was his collaboration with Stanley Kubrick on *Paths of Glory*, which is more interesting than his work on *The Killing*. I wasn't entirely sure what his precise contributions had been, but I found myself strongly drawn to a particular section of the film: the conspiracy among the generals, the cynical Menjou–Macready scenes. They struck me as far more compelling than the pathos-laden story of the victimised soldiers. To this day, I remain uncertain about the exact contributions of each figure involved: Humphrey Cobb, who wrote the original novel; Thompson; Calder Willingham, a gifted screenwriter; Kubrick himself; and James B. Harris, the creatively involved producer. It's clear all five had a hand in shaping the film, but rightly or wrongly, I saw in my favourite part of the film the distinct hand of Jim Thompson.

Before meeting Thompson, I knew nothing of his personal situation. There was a photograph of him on the back cover of a Série noire edition, showing a man who looked to be about 50 or 55, but when I finally saw him in person, I was struck by how aged and worn he looked—prematurely so. He was living in Los Angeles, in a dilapidated house at the top of Whitey Avenue, not far from Musso & Frank's. He could make his way down the hill, but not always back up. It became clear very quickly that he drank too much. Our first meeting went well and we arranged to meet again the followed day at a Polynesian restaurant called Luao. There were two locations, one in Hollywood, the other in Beverly Hills. We were meant to meet at the Beverly Hills branch, but Thompson went to the one in Hollywood. After waiting for half an hour, I figured out the misunderstanding, called him, and rushed over. By the time I arrived, he was already drunk. You couldn't leave him alone in a bar.

By then, Jim Thompson's finest work was already behind him. He had slipped into obscurity.

He had just finished a novelization of *Nothing But a Man*, Michael Roemer's film, and had worked on the TV series *Ironside* and on *The Undefeated*, Andrew McLaglen's Western starring John Wayne and Rock Hudson. He was writing on spec, a practice I hadn't known about at the time. He would write thirty pages or so and send them to publishers. If they showed interest, he would get a contract. Of the three samples I read, the most compelling eventually became *Child of Rage*. At the time it was called *White Mother, Black Son*. I immediately saw its potential, not just as a bold and searing novel but as a remarkable film. He had also been writing short stories. I pitched these novels to the Série noire publisher Gallimard, and they began to appear after 1967. At one point, I even owned the only existing copy of *A Hell of a Woman*. Whenever I visited

Hollywood, I made a point of seeing him. He confided a great deal, telling me that he admired James B. Harris but spoke bitterly of Kubrick, accusing him of having cheated him out of screen credit for *Paths of Glory* and *The Killing*. He also resented the financial terms Kubrick had imposed. Harris, he always insisted, had been fair; Kubrick had not. He particularly regretted the fate of *Lunatic at Large*, a project which had been shelved. I read the script, which was extraordinary. It could have made a great film. At the time, since Kubrick wasn't going to direct it, the project might have ended up in the hands of Richard Fleischer, Don Siegel or Gordon Douglas.

Thompson liked to say that all his novels were Marxist. The greatest book ever written, he told me, was *Don Quixote*. Time and again, he returned to Cervantes, claiming that his own novels shared something with Cervantes' epic—namely, that nothing is ever quite what it seems. He returned to this idea constantly.

What were his living conditions like?

He lived with his wife, son, and, I think, one of his daughters, and at one point confided to me that he had kept a mistress in New York. His marriage, he said, was a ruin. There was no intimacy, no communication—perhaps there never had been. His wife was devoutly Catholic, and after bearing three children, she refused to have any more. And since she refused to use contraceptives, she made him undergo a vasectomy. I think you can read *The Nothing Man* through the lens of that episode—as a novel about impotence.

His wife once told me she had never read a single line of his work, and he lived with the knowledge that he had not received the recognition he deserved. If Thompson and I got on, it was because he was so lonely. He saw very few people, apart from the filmmaker and screenwriter Vernon Zimmerman; Mike Medavoy, his agent at the time—though their relationship lacked the ease and intimacy he shared with Jerry Bick, a successful film producer. Bick, along with Albert Niego, a waiter at the old Musso & Frank Grill in Hollywood, was one of the few people Thompson always spoke of with affection.

Bick, for his part, began as a literary agent and later became a film agent, representing screenwriters, the best-known of whom was Thompson. Later, he took a particular interest in Daniel Mainwaring, whose literary gifts he greatly admired. Bick's name surfaced frequently in my conversations with Thompson. There was a kind of kinship between them, a friendship between two kindred spirits.

Child of Rage, one of Thompson's last novels, and among his finest, is dedicated to you. Under what circumstances was it written?

I had persuaded Claude Chabrol's producer, André Génovès, to finance the writing of *Child of Rage*. Thompson had just received an advance for the film rights to *The Getaway*, and Vernon Zimmerman and Tony Bill had optioned *Texas by the Tail*. I thought it best that Thompson come to Paris, which he did in 1972. That was a wild adventure. My idea was for him to write the novel away from the distractions of his family life. I thought removing him from his domestic environment might give him the space and clarity he needed.

Things quickly became chaotic. We had to change his hotel every day. He and Alfred Eibel, who was thrilled to meet him, had drunk so much that they unbolted a sink from the bathroom wall and hurled it out the window. The receptionist called a few hours later to say they no longer wanted Thompson as a guest. He had defecated in the bidet. Two days later, Thompson received a telegram from his wife saying that their son had attempted suicide. Needless to say, he wrote nothing while he was in Paris. Several months later, he began working on the novel back home in Los Angeles. I stayed involved throughout, helping him recapture the taut style of his best work. Behind the scenes, I tried to remain true to Thompson's spirit. He had been tempted to tone down the violence and boldness of the book, but I encouraged him to go straight for the jugular. He thought that by softening things, the novel might be more commercial.

Why was Child of Rage *never adapted into a film? This was, after all, a time—the mid-1970s—when Thompson was experiencing something of a revival in Hollywood after the success of* The Getaway.

The subject of the book—a boy abused by his mother who takes revenge on others in a completely cynical way—its violence and its rawness, scared people off. I really thought it would entice a few filmmakers. I approached Roger Corman to produce the adaptation, then Don Siegel, but then Siegel finally got the chance to make *The Beguiled*, and it didn't do well. The same thing happened with *Charley Varrick*, and Siegel went on to make *Telefon* with Charles

Bronson and *Rough Cut* with Burt Reynolds. He may have been losing his touch. He had stopped fighting.

Jerry Bick's name comes up frequently among the people you mention. Who was he, apart from being Jim Thompson's agent?

I met Jerry through the agent George Litto, who represented Robert Altman, Abraham Polonsky, Waldo Salt, Michael Wilson and, as I discovered too late, Alfred Hayes. Over time, Jerry and I developed a bond rooted in shared literary tastes. Jerry was always ahead of the curve—championing James Salter or Richard Ford before anyone else. John Ford said Jerry Bick was the most impressive person he had met in Hollywood.

A second-hand book sale mattered more to Jerry than a studio meeting. He really should have become a major studio executive. He introduced me to a number of writers, including L. Steni—a physician by trade who wrote very little, but whose novels were extraordinary. His three finest works are *Prelude to a Rope for Myer*, *Soldier Adrift* and *Afternoon and Twilight of Vanda Pinelli*, which is the story of a doctor in a displaced persons camp after the Second World War. *Prelude to a Rope for Myer* is about a Jew awaiting execution, tracing his way back through his Jewishness, the threads of society, and his own life.

At one point, Jerry turned to producing. His best-known films are *The Long Goodbye* and *Thieves Like Us*, both directed by Robert Altman. Without him, neither Alain Corneau nor Bertrand Tavernier would have had access to the rights to *Pop. 1280* or *A Hell of a Woman*. Jerry was a deeply cultured, sensitive man, a dreamer at heart, he was drawn more to conversation with writers and the re-reading of great books than to climbing Hollywood's greasy pole. He would hand out photocopies of Edward Anderson's *Hungry Men* to people he liked and could discuss Jean Prévost's *La Création chez Stendhal* with real insight. He produced *Michael Kohlhaas* for Volker Schlöndorff, based on Kleist's novel. The film may not have been entirely successful, but that's another story. Jerry was never Raymond Chandler's agent, but he remained close to Chandler's heirs and, for a time, held the rights to some of his short stories.

Which is why he produced The Long Goodbye *for Altman.*

I believe there's something of Jerry in *The Long Goodbye*. He and Altman were very close at the time. The iconoclastic decision to cast Elliott Gould as Philip Marlowe was a product of their shared vision. The conversations between Altman and Bick were on a whole other level than those Altman had with other producers. Curiously, *The Long Goodbye* draws more from Boris Vian's French translation than from Chandler's original. The film, with its blend of irony, nostalgia, and tenderness, doesn't have a very Chandleresque spirit. Marlowe appears out of step with the world, unlike the versions played by Dick Powell or Humphrey Bogart. Jerry Bick, too, was out of step, but unlike Altman, he didn't know how to fight back. The idea of structuring a film around its musical theme came from Altman.

Jerry's second collaboration with Altman, *Thieves Like Us*, is more faithful to Edward Anderson's novel than Nicholas Ray's *They Live by Night* had been, but Jerry was still unhappy with the result. I think he quietly wished the film had been closer to Rowland Brown's earlier, unrealised adaptation. One might think Altman, sensing Jerry's disappointment, distanced himself out of fear of failure. Altman would go on to make many fine films, but he never quite blossomed in the way one might have hoped.

Did you work on any projects with Jerry Bick?

We tried to get an adaptation of Chandler's *The Lady in the Lake* going with Elliott Kastner. There were two existing scripts, neither quite ready, so we planned to synthesise them into a more viable draft, but none of the directors we approached wanted to take it on. I still believe that it wouldn't have taken much to convince Sean Connery to be in the film.

When you first met Clint Eastwood, he was already the star of Leone's westerns and a somewhat controversial figure, though not yet the filmmaker he would become. What was your impression of him?

I met him through Jennings Lang. I had admired *For a Few Dollars More* and *The Good, the Bad and the Ugly*, and I had met Sergio Leone. I also knew Don Siegel. Eastwood and I had lunch at Marius et Jeannette before *The Beguiled* had been completed, and I was struck by his sense of humour. I sensed there was more to him. Less self-assured than other actors I had met, he was almost shy—more curious, more open. The lunch went very well, and he offered me the use of his office whenever I was in Los Angeles.

What cemented your friendship with him?

The Beguiled was a flop in America, but he had produced it, pushed it through at Universal, and sensed that Siegel could make it into his best film. Many people back off when a film fails, but Clint immediately stood by *The Beguiled*, as he would later with *Breezy*, *Bronco Billy* and *Honkytonk Man*. In France, where I handled the release, *The Beguiled* was both a critical and commercial success. Clint also appreciated that, at a time when few took him seriously, I didn't see him as some kind of idiot.

How did you react when you learned he was going to direct?

When he told me he was going to direct *Play Misty for Me* himself, I was apprehensive, but then I was witness to a revealing little moment between him and Jessica Walter that changed my mind. I had gone to meet Clint at his office. He hadn't arrived yet—he often kept people waiting—and Jessica was there, casually sketching a portrait while she waited. She clearly saw herself in the role, which surprised me, since I knew the character and hadn't imagined her that way. When Clint finally showed up, the three of us chatted informally for a while. I could tell that he had already decided she was the one he wanted.

In *Play Misty for Me*, Clint played a man quite unlike the persona the public had come to expect. Erotic tension has always been present in his work—even in his later films, where it gives way to a calmer, more settled tone. I found *Play Misty for Me* uneven, but the scenes with Jessica were much more compelling than those with Donna Mills.

In that film, without seeming to, he managed to evoke a deep tenderness, a quiet melancholy. *Breezy* already reveals Clint's intimate side, which would later surface in *Bird*, *The Bridges of Madison County* and *Million Dollar Baby*. In *The Bridges of Madison County*, the scene in which Clint and Meryl Streep pass each other in their cars and are forced to pretend they don't see one another is miraculous. What everyone recognises today is still a lesson for us all: to stay alert and as open as we can be.

The Outlaw Josey Wales was better received, but Clint never understood the hostility directed at him. The accusations of fascism baffled him, as did being branded right-wing, particularly in the American context, where that label doesn't mean much anymore. The same was said of John Ford, a conservative who made *The Grapes of Wrath*.

Clint took composer Jerry Fielding off the blacklist without caring whether he was left-wing or not, and from early on, there were more black and hispanic crew members on his sets than in the average union crews. His conduct on set is more democratic and fraternal than that of some filmmakers and actors who loudly proclaim their liberalism. Yes, Clint is a conservative, and he showed that again recently with his rather silly "empty chair" sketch directed at Obama, towards whom he had developed an inexplicable aversion. But he immediately railed against Bush's invasion of Iraq. Things are never as simplistic as ideologues claim. I sensed from the first moment that he wasn't the reactionary cowboy people took him for, though I could never have imagined he would go on to be the filmmaker he is today.

For years, Eastwood maintained a uniquely close relationship with Don Siegel, far more so than with Sergio Leone. He made five films with Siegel, from Coogan's Bluff *to* Escape from Alcatraz. *How do you explain their relationship?*

Siegel was efficient in every sense. He worked quickly, directly, without wasting time or words, and that suited Clint. They also shared a similar ironic, often biting sense of humour, and both kept a certain distance from the studio system. Even their way of speaking about women—at times admiring, at times less so—reflected a shared outlook, however dated. That sort of bond never existed between Eastwood and Leone. There was the language barrier, of course, but even without it, the same kind of relationship would never have developed.

When did Eastwood finally shed the "pseudo-fascist" label that had clung to him for so long?

In the mid 1980s, with *Tightrope* and *Pale Rider*. When *Tightrope* came out, Joe Hyams—who looked after Clint and Stanley Kubrick at Warners—asked me to support the film and help reshape Eastwood's image in the press. That was when we organised a retrospective at the Cinémathèque française. I wrote an accompanying essay, trying to show that Clint wasn't the man so many had assumed him to be. The event was a success, and *Pale Rider* was selected for Cannes.

Would you say that Bird *marked another artistic turning point in Eastwood's career?*

Even when it was first released, *Bird*—which may be, for me, his greatest film—wasn't universally embraced. That came with *Unforgiven*. What I managed to do for Clint in France and then in Europe, I began to replicate in America with *Bird*. At the time, only a few isolated voices there were speaking up in his defence.

Eventually you no longer had to defend him and began working more proactively with him.

I played a role in Clint's decision to direct *Letters from Iwo Jima*, which remains his most "auteur"-like film. It didn't begin with a script. While preparing *Flags of Our Fathers*, he had the idea of telling the same story from the Japanese side. He commissioned the project and kept a close eye on the script's development.

Clint kept pestering me—if I can put it that way—asking who the "Kurosawa of today" might be, the contemporary Japanese director who could take on the project. I couldn't think of anyone, so I finally suggested he direct it himself. "You really think I should?" he asked. "Yes," I said. "There's a better chance it will be a great film than if you hand it to some journeyman Japanese director." I wouldn't presume to say the idea hadn't crossed his mind already, but it was after that phone call that he made up his mind.

Clint has chosen to make films that are fully his own. He wants to keep filming. He has no career anxieties, no financial worries. He has received every honour. He has it all. So what's left? New films. That's his final frontier.

Changeling, Hereafter and American Sniper, his more recent films, have not always been universally praised.

I'm very fond of *Changeling*, which contains some of the most beautiful scenes Eastwood has ever filmed. *Hereafter* also has moments that are quite remarkable. It may not be a perfect film, but Matt Damon brings such humility and precision, and the scenes with the twins are beautiful. Every one of Eastwood's films contains sequences of real brilliance. As for *American Sniper*, aside from the usual silly questions about whether it glorifies war or fetishises soldiers, even his detractors have had to admit that Clint's direction is masterful.

You once had a documentary project on Eastwood. What aspects of his personality would you have wanted to explore?

I wanted to show how deeply he's a child of the Great Depression. His parents' wandering years gave him a first-hand sense of America as a place where people clung to whatever sliver of opportunity they could find. That, to me, is why he remains the only contemporary director who can still make Westerns in the traditional sense—films in the spirit of Anthony Mann, Delmer Daves, Ford and Walsh.

Clint was born in 1930 and moved around constantly. He did all sorts of odd jobs. He carries within him that idea of heading out west, the dream of building something better just over the horizon. That's the core of *The Outlaw Josey Wales*, just as it's at the heart of Anthony Mann's *Bend of the River* and *The Far Country*, and even Ford's *The Grapes of Wrath*, which isn't a Western but spiritually belongs to the same tradition. That legacy is embedded in Clint, just like his deep understanding of the black experience, which is so palpable in *Bird* and which stems from his early immersion, as a young man, in the world of jazz clubs.

Were there filmmakers you knew well but never quite understood?

John Huston is a special case. Always affable, always attentive, but at the same time, you felt him to be very distant. He was driven by curiosity, pleasure and self-interest, and in the end I would be hard-pressed to say who Huston really was, except that he was elusive. Most people who knew him from the 1950s onward seem to have felt the same way. The most surprising thing about him is that his filmmaking kept evolving. His early films had a sharpness, certainly much more than people admitted during the heyday of Hitchcocko-Hawkism or the Mac-Mahon circle. A film like *Wise Blood*, which is perhaps his best, is really quite extraordinary. The only time I felt a kind of real affinity with Huston was in his sense of irony, the idea that nothing should be taken too seriously. He had his own code, his own way of measuring the world. He had seen a lot, and that gave him an air of both casualness and elegance that kept you at arm's length.

I'm still moved by the memory of a lunch I had with him and Suzanne Flon. As surprising as it may seem, everyone knows she was the great love of his life. At the end of a morning of interviews, Huston told me he was going to have lunch with her. "I'll be back at three," I said. "No," he replied, "stay." So I did. I saw them together: no declarations, no excessive words, no hand-holding, not even a meaningful look, but such love, still so alive after all those years. Having since experienced such feelings myself, I know that on that day, I came closer to John Huston than any confession might ever have allowed.

You also knew Romy Schneider.

I had met her briefly once, but it was only during the shooting of *La Piscine*, when I was working as a press attaché alongside Jacques Deray, that I really got to know her. She told me she was turning down scripts in order to devote herself to François Reichenbach's first fiction film. I flippantly asked her which script she had just rejected. It turned out to be the next film by someone whose name she barely recognised: Claude Sautet. I jumped, and told her, with some urgency, that Sautet was a filmmaker she should follow almost blindly. As admirable as Reichenbach was as a documentarian, there was simply no comparison between the two. She didn't seem convinced, but in the end I managed to persuade her. I'm glad that evening led to *Les Choses de la vie* and *Max et les Ferrailleurs,* which contains one of her greatest performances, and is one of Sautet's most intimate films.

In time, Romy began to trust me, and we spent a great deal of time together. More than once, she asked for my opinion on scripts and directors. I have a few regrets. I had sent her Jim Thompson's short story *Then the Fireworks,* which she loved. I also passed it along to Jean Renoir, who showed interest, but he already had another project in mind — one that, in the end, never happened. If Renoir had been available, at the height of his powers, and with Romy in the lead, it might have been a magnificent film.

That was a period when I was starting to travel a great deal. My absences became more frequent, and I began to lose touch with many of my friends. I remember a vibrant evening with Howard Hawks, whose wit Romy matched with ease. She had a zest for life and wanted to work with interesting directors, but circumstances didn't always align. I was no longer much in contact with her when she died, which I deeply regret. She had a passionate, almost feverish emotional energy.

MEMORIES OF OUR FATHERS: FORGOTTEN FILMMAKERS

Your passion for cinema has taken you to new territories in Asia and the Americas. This voyage through space is inseparable from a journey through time. For you, film history remains largely uncharted land.

Before I discovered Asia, I had already immersed myself in film history beyond what had been uncovered or rediscovered in the 1950s. I still remember how stunned I was by Leo McCarey's *Love Affair* when I finally saw it around 1972. By then, it had become almost impossible to find. I was encountering filmmakers like Hanns Schwarz and his wonderful 1937 film *The Lie of Nina Petrovna*. Schwarz was a truly great director. That discovery also gave me a different perspective on Max Ophüls, who we tended to see as a solitary figure, but it's very likely he saw *Nina Petrovna*, which was a big success when it was released.

Schwarz is largely absent from most film histories. How did you come across him?

I stumbled across a small booklet containing an interview with the German producer Erich Pommer in which he mentioned his two favourite films, one by Ludwig Berger from 1925, apparently lost, and *Nina Petrovna*. Who wouldn't be intrigued? Erich Pommer was the producer behind Murnau and Lang at UFA, and yet Schwarz wasn't even listed in film dictionaries. Eventually, in 1972, I was able to see the film in a 9.5mm print that ran just fifty-two minutes. I was dazzled. Later, John Gillett, one of the programmers at the British Film Institute, found a more complete print in London. Whenever I had the opportunity, I programmed it in festivals and retrospectives.

What do you know about Hanns Schwarz?

Very little. He came from the theatre and made only a handful of films. The first one I saw was *Hungarian Rhapsody*. *Nina Petrovna* is a film of remarkable modesty, though it is directed with such delicacy and control that its precision becomes almost invisible. The film is like a razor's edge that scrapes the skin of its characters, laying bare their nerves. With every shot, you feel as if you've cut yourself on a shard of broken glass.

　　Schwarz later made a film in France with Jean Gabin, *Cœurs Joyeux*, which is no masterpiece. Some say that Jacques Tourneur may have contributed to it. Then he moved to England, where he directed two films:, one with

Ida Lupino called *Prince of Arcadia*, of which no known print exists, and another, quite mediocre film, *Return of the Scarlet Pimpernel*. Around that time, he left for America, though it took him years to get there because he was stuck in Mexio waiting for his visa. Apparently he had a project underway there, but no trace of it remains. He finally arrived in America in 1943 and died of cancer in 1945, aged 55. He had adopted an American pseudonym, Howard Shelton, and is said to have worked for the U.S. Army.

This notion of a thwarted destiny—when the career of a gifted filmmaker is cut short and they fall into obscurity—seems important to you.

Absolutely. Gustav Machatý comes to mind. There's the famous film of his, *Ecstasy*, which was a tremendous critical and public success. It had an enormous impact before the war; Henry Miller even wrote about it. How is it that someone with such talent, and who had enjoyed such acclaim, could all but vanish? The film was still being shown in Paris as late as 1954, but in a butchered version, and it left me more disappointed than impressed. Apart from *Erotikon*, none of Machatý's other films are known, so I had completely forgotten his name when, by chance, during a retrospective of Czech cinema in London, I had the opportunity to see *From Saturday to Sunday*. That film, released in 1931, is in my view the first truly great sound film. I was dazzled and deeply moved by this discreet, modest work, which radiates a profound vulnerability, like an open wound. And it's set in Prague, not Paris, Berlin, or New York. The fact that such a masterpiece could come from a seemingly "minor" national cinema makes it all the more astonishing.

I later discovered that the screenplay had been written by Vítězslav Nezval, a leading Czech poet. His sensibility runs through every aspect of the film—its characters, its setting, its evocation of city and night. That discovery transformed my view of Machatý entirely. One thing that struck me in particular was the film's emotional tone, which feels astonishingly close to Jean Vigo's *L'Atalante*. There's no narrative resemblance, but there is something similar in spirit and tone. Since *Erotikon* had been a great favourite of the surrealists at Studio 28, it's quite likely that Vigo saw *From Saturday to Sunday*.

The film Machatý went on to make in Vienna, *Nocturno*, is very curious and shows a keen sense of mise en scène. The sets aren't just decorative—they're inhabited by the actors and permeated with the film's atmosphere. By contrast, *Ballerine* has a terrible reputation, sadly quite deserved. It's really quite foolish. It was Machatý's last film in Europe before returning much later under rather tragic circumstances. He had signed a contract in America with MGM, likely on the strength of *Ecstasy*, but it's said that the failure of *Ballerine* at the Venice Film Festival was reported back to Louis B. Mayer, and the deal fell through. Machatý ended up working on second unit crews for big productions. He directed a short in the *Crime Doesn't Pay* series called *The Wrong Way Out*, which was actually quite good, and eventually got the chance to direct a feature: *Within the Law*, a low-budget film with an odd opening credit sequence and dialogue reportedly rewritten afterward by Charles Lederer. It's nothing more than a routine B-picture.

Something must have happened. There were even whispers that he worked for the military. In any case, Machatý didn't direct for the studios again until 1945, when he made *Jealousy* for Republic Studios. Dalton Trumbo told me he had helped with the screenplay as a favour to Machatý. I regret not having seen the film early enough to discuss it with him. I came across it in a very poor 16mm print, and my impression was lukewarm. I would be very curious to see it again today. The great writer and screenwriter James Agee took an interest in it, and it's also one of the very few films for which Hanns Eisler composed a score.

After that, Machatý stopped working again. I wonder what his life was like until his wife's suicide in 1951, which prompted his sudden departure back to Europe. He settled in Hamburg and in 1955 made a film called *Suchkind 312*. He clearly didn't have the equipment he needed. It's competently directed but basically has no soundtrack. Machatý later worked in radio, either in Munich or Prague, and died in 1963, never having managed to stage a comeback.

Another compelling case is that of d'Abbadie d'Arrast. Under what circumstances did you take an interest in him?

I barely knew his name when, by chance, I came across a long piece about him in Herman G. Weinberg's book *Coffee, Brandy, and Cigars*. But the article never asked the key question: why did this filmmaker—who apparently had everything going for him—stop working? Henri—who anglicised his name to Harry—d'Abbadie d'Arrast was born in 1897 in Buenos Aires, where his father, a Basque nobleman from the small village of Saint-Étienne-de-Baïgorry, had built the city's tramway network. He had a sister, and a brother who was killed in the First World War in 1917. I managed to track down a few elderly villagers who remembered the family's return to France when Henri was still a boy. He received an excellent education at the Lycée Janson-de-Sailly in Paris, also possibly in England and perhaps even Switzerland. After his brother's death, he enlisted in the army and suffered a serious wound to his arm. A cutting-edge surgical procedure of the time restored some mobility, but the injury troubled him for the rest of his life and worsened with age. After the war, he settled in Paris. There were rumours that, along with a Spanish nobleman named Ricardo Soriano, he helped develop a new automobile—the Soriano—which my father vaguely recalled. It was in Paris that he met George Fitzmaurice, a leading Hollywood director of the time. Fitzmaurice, half Irish and half French, was a refined gourmet and often travelled to France because he liked its restaurants. He was struck by d'Arrast's wit and encouraged him to come to Hollywood. D'Arrast made the journey and, with his aristocratic title, quickly became a figure of fascination in social circles. He even made brief appearances in two films starring Gloria Swanson, directed by Jack Conway. Henry Hathaway, who had been an assistant on those films, still remembered him.

When Chaplin began preparing *A Woman of Paris*, he surrounded himself with four assistants: two Americans, Monta Bell and Eddie Sutherland, and two Frenchmen, d'Arrast and Jean de Limur, whom I had the chance to meet when he was 87. One wonders whether d'Arrast had a hand in shaping Adolphe Menjou's finely shaded performance as a French aristocrat. A behind-the-scenes photo shows him seated beside Chaplin, watching Menjou with intense focus. D'Arrast remained close to Chaplin, and his name appears in the credits for *The Gold Rush*, with the prominent credit of assistant director. Chaplin even visited Saint-Étienne-de-Baïgorry twice during that time. Louise Brooks once recalled seeing the two of them together in New York. It seems they were practically inseparable.

D'Arrast's company was increasingly sought after in Hollywood. He was hired by Marion Davies, the mistress of press baron William Randolph Hearst, to develop a film of which no trace remains, and made his directorial debut in 1927 at Paramount with *Service for Ladies*, starring Adolphe Menjou. The film is now lost, but those who saw it remembered it with wonder, and Alexander Korda remade it in 1932. In quick succession, d'Arrast directed three more films for Paramount and one for Fox called *Dry Martini*. A photograph shows him among the company of Murnau,

Borzage, Walsh and Ford — some of the era's most celebrated directors. His reputation was such that Maurice Chevalier asked him to direct *Innocents of Paris*, but d'Arrast declined after reading the script. A surprising move, perhaps, from a director whose output was largely made up of drawing-room comedies. Monta Bell, who had taken over the Astoria Paramount studios in New York, invited him to join Walter Wanger and Herman Mankiewicz, who would go on to produce *Laughter*, d'Arrast's first talkie. Donald Ogden Stewart, an up and coming young playwright, wrote the script, and the film featured one of stage actor Fredric March's first roles. Glenn Anders, another theatre performer, later seen in small parts for Welles and Losey, is remarkable as a deeply troubled character, a poor artist driven to suicide by hopeless love. The film has a remarkably bold ending for its time. It was a critical success and is still often cited as the first American comedy. D'Arrast was ahead of Gregory La Cava, Leo McCarey and George Cukor.

Why didn't he achieve their level of success?

Did he come to France to work on a film made by former schoolmates from Janson-de-Sailly — aristocrats like himself? The film, now lost, was titled *Sous le casque de cuir* and was officially attributed to Albert de Courville. But Roger de Saint-Affrique, a cousin of d'Arrast, believed it was actually directed by d'Arrast himself, even though there is no proof of this. I wrote to the film's stars, Pierre Richard-Willm and Gina Manès, to ask them, but never received a reply. Or did he first direct *Raffles* for Samuel Goldwyn, with Ronald Colman? And if so, how long was he actually on set before an argument erupted between Goldwyn and d'Arrast. Did he walk off or was he fired?

What is certain is that he was back in Paris when Lewis Milestone — riding high from *All Quiet on the Western Front* — was appointed head of production at United Artists. Milestone invited d'Arrast back to Hollywood, and he returned to work on a screenplay he had conceived with Ben Hecht called *The New Yorker*. Al Jolson, star of *The Jazz Singer*, was cast in the lead and would have received the highest salary ever offered to a star at the time.

But just days before filming was to begin, after some rehearsal sessions, d'Arrast went to Milestone and announced he no longer wanted to make the film with Jolson. He preferred an actor he had just discovered in a musical vaudeville who he felt was a better fit for the role. Milestone was stunned because he fought tooth and

nail to get d'Arrast approved by the powerful producer
Joe Schenck. Whether d'Arrast resigned or was fired is
unclear. *The New Yorker*, taken over by Milestone and
retitled *Hallelujah, I'm a Bum*, flopped at the box office
and derailed Jolson's career. The actor d'Arrast had wanted
instead became an overnight sensation. His name was Fred
Astaire. D'Arrast's only fault, in this case, was being right
too soon.

He used to say he had turned down twenty-nine film
offers, all of which later flopped. There were rumours that
Walter Wanger wanted him for *Queen Christina*, which
went instead to Rouben Mamoulian. His name also came up
in connection with Dashiell Hammett's *The Glass Key* and
with a play by Marcel Achard, *La Vie est belle*, whose rights
d'Arrast purchased under the patronage of Ernst Lubitsch,
then head of production at Paramount. Alongside Donald
Ogden Stewart and Edgar Neville, a Spanish nobleman
working at his country's consulate, he began adapting the
play for the screen.

But his difficult temperament increasingly isolated him.
He refused to cut costs, wouldn't speed up the shooting
schedule, and soon found himself at odds with studios and
producers. Eventually he left for Spain, where, with financing
from his friend Ricardo Soriano and writing support from
Edgar Neville—who had by then become an important
playwright and would go on to become a leading Spanish
filmmaker—d'Arrast directed *La travesía molinera*. It was
shot in three versions—Spanish, French and English—the
first of which became the country's biggest hit at the time.
Both Lorca and Chaplin reportedly admired it. And yet
every print and the original negative have vanished. Douglas
Fairbanks and Mary Pickford purchased international rights
through United Artists, but Schenck, still nursing a grudge,
ensured the film was never released outside Spain.

What followed remains somewhat murky. D'Arrast
developed a project for Mary Pickford. In London, he
spent considerable time preparing a *Cyrano de Bergerac*
adaptation written by Ben Hecht for Alexander Korda. He
drifted through the late 1930s and early '40s between Biarritz
and Nice, before returning to America in 1942. Lewis
Milestone told me that by then, d'Arrast had lost interest in
filmmaking and was a regular at the racetracks instead. Still,
at least two unfulfilled projects remain known: a remake of
Les Musiciens du ciel, based on a novel by René Lefèvre,
and *The Emperor's Foot*, later retitled *Quixote Rides Again*,
briefly in development at RKO around 1950. Edgar Neville
tried to convince him to return to simpler projects in Spain,

but by then d'Arrast's mind seemed elsewhere. A heart-wrenching letter from the 1960s reveals his infatuation with a much younger woman—Neville's secretary—and of a life spinning in circles, empty and aimless.

Why did he stop making films? George Falsey, his cinematographer on *Laughter*, once said that d'Arrast was antisemitic and that this had led to his blacklisting by Hollywood studios. For a time, I believed this, but I've come to a more nuanced view. His closest friends—Ben Hecht, Herman Mankiewicz, Joe Cohn, Harpo Marx, with whom he tried to launch a *Sergeant York* project, Lewis Milestone, Sidney Buchman, Alexander Korda—were all Jewish, and they admired him deeply. I think the truth is that he had extremely fragile nerves, a mix of pride and shyness. Henry Hathaway once told me, "He was stubborn, but not tough." George Cukor said, simply, "He was an amateur." As for Joseph L. Mankiewicz, he felt d'Arrast simply didn't belong in the Hollywood jungle.

He was obsessively meticulous, down to the last detail, and argued bitterly with anyone who disagreed—producers, stars, even moguls like Goldwyn, Schenck and Thalberg. Perhaps, given that he was raised an aristocrat, he knew the worst kinds of anti-Jewish insults and used them not for ideological reasons but just as insults. He spent his final years in Monte Carlo, reportedly gambling away his wife's money. He died of a sudden stroke in 1968. Only in 1972 did *Laughter*, *Topaze* and *A Gentleman of Paris* resurface, sparking renewed interest among cinephiles.

Just as Hanns Schwarz anticipates Ophüls, do you see other overlooked connections between filmmakers in cinema history?

I discovered Anatole Litvak's *Nie wieder Liebe* rather late. Max Ophüls was first assistant director and Franz Planer was the cinematographer. The film's elegant, gliding movements seem to foreshadow *Liebelei*, Ophüls' first major work. Could Litvak have let Ophüls direct certain scenes? I doubt it. What's more likely is that Ophüls absorbed a great deal on that set, just as he must have been profoundly struck by Erik Charell's *Der Kongreß tanzt*. That film was a sensation, and Charell was swiftly brought to Hollywood, where he directed *Caravan* in 1934, a critical and commercial failure that ended his directing career. And yet *Caravan* is dazzling. The camera movements, the fluidity of the mise en scène—it's impossible not to think of Ophüls. One might also wonder whether it was really Preminger who first worked extensively with the crane, because if Charell didn't have a crane, how on earth did he film some of those sequences in *Caravan*? There's no doubt that a particular Weimar aesthetic binds these filmmakers. Shame on Hitler and Goebbels for destroying it.

On the subject of silent cinema—so often encrusted with myth—one sometimes gets the impression it all began with D. W. Griffith's The Birth of a Nation *in 1915.*

But Griffith had already existed long before that film. Several shorts and medium-length features attest to that. His importance is perhaps comparable to that of *Citizen Kane*, in the sense that both marked a moment when audiences became vividly aware of a shift, when the medium itself suddenly felt new. And yet, when people talk about the influence of Welles, I challenge them to name films that were truly influenced by *Kane* in the years that followed. At most, they can point to a few stylistic quirks here and there, but those are the least important aspects of film direction. And let's not forget that *Kane*, too, had its forerunners. Welles watched dozens of films with Gregg Toland, his cinematographer, including John Ford's films, with whom Toland had collaborated.

Before Griffith, or during the same period, have you identified other filmmakers of real significance?

I would name five. The first is Urban Gad, the Danish filmmaker who directed *Afgrunden* in 1909, starring Asta Nielsen. I've seen several of his films from 1910 and 1911, and they are even more compelling. Gad's cinema doesn't depend on montage. Typically, there's just one shot per scene, framed in a way that might seem conventional on the surface, but the miracle lies in the spatial composition, the camera angle, the lens choice, and a crisp quality of light unique to the film stock of the time.

Another director now being rediscovered is Albert Capellani, whose many films predate *The Birth of a Nation*. Many of his scenes are mired in theatrical conventions, but his images have a real power when capturing landscapes, streets and astonishingly truthful characters. This is especially true in *Les Misérables, Quatre-vingt-treize, L'Assommoir* and *Germinal*. Capellani is likely the most important French silent filmmaker, alongside Léonce Perret, who also deserves serious attention for *L'Enfant de Paris* and a few other remarkable works.

The third figure I would highlight is Raymond Longford, an Australian filmmaker whose work has been tragically lost. He may have been the first true casualty of American cultural imperialism in the realm of cinema. Between 1924 and 1926, the Hollywood majors inundated the Australian market with their own productions and bought out the local cinemas, leading to the collapse of what had been a flourishing national industry. All that remains of *The Romantic Story of Margaret Catchpole* is a single surviving sequence, but in that one shot, with a single camera movement, Longford manages to evoke not only a trembling in the air but a profound sense of the characters' presence within their environment. A brief interview that Longford gave to Australian television when he was 84 and by then working as a dockyard watchman to survive leaves on longing for more.

Finally, I would mention Cecil B. DeMille. His work, even before *The Birth of a Nation*, was already of real consequence. *What's His Name* is especially striking in its realism and the cruelty it shows towards its characters. His body of work, both in terms of style and of theme, is far more surprising than the popular image of him suggests. Though he was already politically conservative, his films about morality and gender relations might just as easily have been made by someone from the opposite side of the ideological spectrum.

Are there other silent filmmakers who deserve rediscovery?

Monta Bell. He worked as Chaplin's assistant on *A Woman of Paris* and went on to direct several fine films of his own: *After Midnight, Upstage* and *Man, Woman and Sin*. In *Upstage*, the attention to detail within the larger dynamics of each scene is extraordinary. The way the film sustains continuity through a sequence feels strikingly modern. Like many of his contemporaries, Bell's career collapsed with the arrival of sound. This is all the more surprising given that the best films of Clarence Badger, Malcolm St. Clair, d'Abbadie d'Arrast and Bell himself might have led one to believe they were among the most ready to transition to sound.

Perhaps it wasn't the revolution of sound that ended their careers. Bell went on to direct two remarkable early talkies: *Young Man of Manhattan*, notable for its startlingly naturalistic performances and its focus on everyday life, and *Downstairs*, which—like Renoir's *The Rules of the Game*—demonstrates a rare sensitivity to social class distinctions in

American cinema. *Downstairs* also dispels the myth spread by Louis B. Mayer, who detested John Gilbert, that Gilbert's voice was unfit for sound. The film proves otherwise. In the end, it seems Bell's downfall was personal, not technical, and that his career was cut short more by his alcoholism than by the coming of sound.

Among silent-era filmmakers who did successfully transition to sound—like Ford or Walsh—which of their silent films are most deserving of rediscovery?

Walsh's *Regeneration*. When it was unearthed by film historians William K. Everson and Alex Gordon, it surprised many with its boldness, vitality and fresh, raw portrayal of reality and character. Walsh had been Griffith's assistant, notably on *The Birth of a Nation*, in which he also played John Wilkes Booth, Abraham Lincoln's assassin. Unfortunately, two films by Walsh that I've heard great things about are now lost: *The Honor System*, set in a prison and described by Ford as the film that had impressed him the most, and *Evangeline*, based on the poem by Henry Wadsworth Longfellow. Walsh told me that after the failure of *Evangeline*, he no longer wanted to make "artistic films," which tells us a lot about what was really important to him. Let's not forget his love of Shakespeare and passion for Stendhal. He wandered the film sets like an adventurer, leaving behind dazzling gems in his wake.

What strikes you most about silent cinema today? Beyond the technical aspects, what defines it in contrast to sound cinema?

Its ability to capture an entire setting—the whole of a village in Capellani, or a cliffside in Raymond Longford's *The Romantic Story of Margaret Catchpole*—and to follow the characters' trajectory through that space. There was a kind of innocence, an instinctive synthesis of cinema's visual powers. In Léonce Perret's films, one senses an immense faith in cinema, as if it believed in itself and directors didn't think of themselves as "authors," even though their personalities were unmistakably present in their films. That initial impulse—the way cinema captured things differently than theatre—was partly lost. You can still feel it in some Westerns, but this loss of innocence pushed cinema to become more intellectual when it should have remained more intuitive. Editing, with its emphasis on continuity and narrative, may have dulled our sense of the moment and of the image as a thing unfolding in real time. In silent cinema, that moment could stretch across the entire film.

How do you explain the sudden disappearance of silent cinema? There's an obvious technical aspect, of course, but it can't explain everything.

It may sound romantic, but I think silent cinema died of its own perfection, its own beauty. One could name several films that give the impression cinema simply couldn't go any further. King Vidor or Frank Borzage, for example, never reached the heights again that they had in their great silent films. What's truly remarkable is how quickly sound cinema asserted itself across different countries. In Germany, there were astonishing films early on: Robert Siodmak's *Abschied* in 1930, written by Emeric Pressburger, and even as early as 1929, with Hanns Schwarz's *Melodie des Herzens*, which was the most advanced film at the time in its conception of sound. There were also brilliant things from Géza von Bolváry; I'm thinking of *Was Frauen träumen*, written by Billy Wilder and featuring Peter Lorre. In Russia, Boris Barnet's *Okraina* was also a surprising exploration of sound, and in France we had Grémillon's *Petite Lise*, Renoir's *La Chienne*, Litvak's *Cœur de lilas* and Feyder's *Le Grand Jeu*, which has an exceptionally modern score by Hanns Eisler.

With the advent of sound, the director's omnipotence was suddenly counterbalanced by that of the screenwriter or dialogue writer.

Nowhere was this shift more visible than in America. A lot of writers—even people who had written just one play, one novel, or one short story, as well as journalists— were hired by the studios with the arrival of sound. This almost spontaneous generation of screenwriters became hugely important, especially at Warner Bros. Some of the most vibrant early sound films emerged from that context, like Wellman's *Other Men's Women* and Walsh's *Me and My Gal*, where the rhythm and bite of the dialogue still feel modern. Howard Hawks once told me, when I asked how he had managed to adapt so quickly and easily to sound, "I just knew how people talk." That reminds me of what William Bowers once told me Dick Powell used to say: "There's nothing mysterious about saying a line. You just say it." Very quickly, people like La Cava and McCarey established themselves as great sound-era directors.

At a recent dinner with Quentin Tarantino, I tried to explain the concept of the cut point, the exact frame where the editor must make the splice. Not a frame before, not a frame after. When working manually on a Steenbeck, each shot has to be "pregnant" with the next. The new image must be born naturally from the previous one. Fritz Lang was both a magician and a master craftsman in this regard. Quentin has an exceptional ear for catching the exact millisecond when a cut should happen or when a line should hit.

THE SPECIALIST: SOME REFLECTIONS ON CINEMA

The question of screenwriting is central to your thinking about cinema and your cinephilia. But when it comes to American cinema of the 1930s and 1940s, it isn't easy to know who the true author of a film's script was.

There are several reasons for that. Producers like Robert Lord, Sidney Buchman and Adrian Scott—who were themselves writers—frequently intervened in the writing process, and there's no doubt they made contributions to the scripts they produced. At the same time, directors like Sternberg, Hawks, McCarey, Capra and La Cava worked closely with their writers. Some films by Jules Furthman — Sternberg's *Morocco* and Hawks' *To Have and Have Not*—share striking similarities in the dialogue and the dynamics between characters, even if those qualities come through in different ways in each film. We should also mention something that people rarely talk about: the phenomenon of the studio commissaries, where individuals from all backgrounds and cultures mingled. They were extraordinary melting pots. Alongside long-established American directors like Hawks, Ford, Walsh and Vidor, you had filmmakers such as Lang, Siodmak, Litvak and Ophüls, and writers of every kind. There wasn't the same atmosphere of envy and animosity that often prevails today; there was more camaraderie. At RKO, for instance, Adrian Scott, Edward Dmytryk, John Berry, Joseph Losey, Hugo Butler, Daniel Mainwaring and Nicholas Ray—all of them progressives—moved within the same creative circles. It's no surprise that RKO, just after the war, was such an innovative studio. When you think about all the filmmakers working at Warner Bros. in the 1930s and the rapid-fire dialogue in their films, you can imagine ideas bouncing around the commissaries, just as they did in the late 1920s at Paramount among directors making sophisticated comedies.

Do you have a favourite screenplay?

Without hesitation: Losey's *The Lawless*, written by Daniel Mainwaring. It was the first time I truly realised that screenplay and direction are inseparable, that mise en scène is simply the natural and transparent outgrowth of the writing. Mainwaring's sensibility was already evident in his novels, even if they now feel somewhat dated in terms of style and genre. He had a magnificent prose style, capable of conjuring the scent of autumn leaves burning in a small-town yard, or the slow, tentative unfolding of love between two people. At the time, Losey shared that same sensibility, which is evident in *The Boy with Green Hair*. Mainwaring's work calls to mind Stendhal's definition of the novel: "a mirror carried along a road," like a tracking shot or pan that follows the characters. The opening lines of *The Street of the Crying Woman*, published under the name Geoffrey Homes, are both simple and deeply poetic. His writing resonates with what moves me most in cinema: intimacy, immediacy, a sense of closeness—like in Walsh's *The Man I Love*. Mainwaring's career wasn't what it might have been, partly because of his gentleness, modesty and lack of ambition, but also due to the chilling effect of McCarthyism. Though never a Communist, the looming threat of blacklisting kept him in a state of paralysing uncertainty, making him wary of long-term commitments. He was one of the very few who presented scripts by blacklisted writers under his own name without asking for a commission. Paul Jarrico told me that Mainwaring submitted his screenplay *Black River* simply out of decency, and when Jarrico finally managed to sell it years later, he insisted on giving Mainwaring a share.

In what other films do you find this relationship between screenplay and mise en scène, where direction becomes the natural and transparent extension of the writing?

In *Cry Danger*, directed by Robert Parrish, written by William Bowers and starring Dick Powell. In this case, screenplay, direction and performance are inseparable. The rapport between Bowers and Powell—who moved through dialogue like a fish in water—made Parrish's work all the more invisible. He let the script breathe, following the rhythm and nuance of the dialogue rather than imposing himself through stylistic flourishes. The exchanges between Powell and Regis Toomey are lightning-fast, intelligent and full of subtle subtext. Powell is a striking example of an actor who, in his laid-back "non-performance," draws on the full depth of his life experience. As a result, you feel like he speaks the way someone really would. It was Raymond Chandler who said that Powell was a better Marlowe than Bogart.

I should also mention Eugene Thackrey, who worked with La Cava on three films, and the dear Alfred Hayes, whose immense talent was sadly underutilised. Or perhaps he allowed himself to become a studio hack. Even so, the episode "A Piece of the Action," written for *The Alfred Hitchcock Hour*, contains some of the most extraordinary dialogue I know of. The brittle relationship between the two brothers, the emotional undercurrents, the pinpoint observations—it's all there, perfectly honed.

In the Mac-Mahonist era, your preferences leaned toward young actors and actresses. How has your taste evolved?

We shouldn't forget that we were all very young ourselves. But it's fair to say now that praising Rhonda Fleming while ignoring Barbara Stanwyck was ridiculous. Even from a romantic point of view, Stanwyck's films are far richer than any featuring Fleming. It was less true for male actors. We admired Richard Widmark and Leo McKern, but probably didn't see Charlton Heston or Fernando Lamas as actors so much as adventure heroes, which is also why we liked Lamas in Edward Ludwig's *Jivaro*, Errol Flynn, who was the quintessential Walshian hero, Douglas Fairbanks in *The Thief of Bagdad*, and Gary Cooper in Walsh's *Distant Drums*.

Errol Flynn may have embodied the swashbuckling hero, but his abilities as an actor went far beyond that.

Watching *Objective, Burma!* again and again, I found myself increasingly struck by Flynn's performance. In my memory, he'd been a kind of smart extra—present, but not essential. I hadn't noticed the precision of his performance and the way his professionalism shapes the film. He rarely gets credit for it. Yet the way he steps back—not just behind the character, but behind the action itself—and the way he blends into the film with a kind of quiet intensity is impressive. It feels strikingly modern. All expressive excess is stripped away; it's a Bressonian performance, but without the abstraction. Flynn acts the way Bresson claimed his performers should act—flat, direct, without underlining their intentions. It's a shame, really. Flynn, a mischievous man in real life, whose wild streak likely kept him from being taken seriously as an actor, died just before *Gentleman Jim* was re-released in France. It's a film that might have restored his standing, if not as a great actor, then at least as a singular presence.

Are there other actor-director pairings you find as fruitful as Walsh and Flynn?

The partnership between Anthony Mann and James Stewart comes immediately to mind, as do Stewart's collaborations with Capra, and to some extent with Hitchcock. *Rope*, certainly, but not *Vertigo*, which I never liked. There is also

Hitchcock and Cary Grant, and Bogart, who was a perfect fit with Huston, Curtiz and Hawks. Certain actors allow directors to flourish, like Adolphe Menjou. Think about what he makes possible in *A Woman of Paris*, *The Front Page* and *Paths of Glory*. There are more recent examples of that same fusion between actor and director, when both are in such close harmony that they give full scope and strength to the script. Early De Niro and Martin Scorsese films are the obvious example. Consider also Siegel with Eastwood and Altman with Michael Murphy and Elliott Gould. In French cinema, the Sautet–Piccoli partnership is unassailable.

Has your view of any actor shifted dramatically over the years?

Charles Boyer. I didn't know his work well, aside from his image as the romantic French seducer in *Conquest*, where he played a rather ridiculous Napoleon. I had seen *The Earrings of Madame de...*, in which I liked him very much, but I still thought he was a poor actor. Then, much later, I saw Leo McCarey's *Love Affair* and was stunned. There was something flowing through him—an extraordinary charm, elegance and grace. From that moment on, I regretted not speaking to him when I encountered him with Fritz Lang in Cannes in 1964, where he also was on the jury. I later learned how cultured he was and that he played a genuine role as an ambassador of French culture in Hollywood. He also had a major theatre career, with roles in Shaw's *Don Juan in Hell* and Sartres' *Les Mains sales*, and had a real connection with Bertolt Brecht. Even when Boyer isn't particularly good, something reveals itself—as if it had emerged from another world, another civilisation, one from the past, yet still astonishingly close.

Another actor I completely changed my opinion on is Gilbert Roland. Like Boyer, I had long dismissed him as ridiculous. And again, as with Boyer, I revised that view. I happened to meet him under rather unusual circumstances, after a screening of Marcel Ophuls' *The Sorrow and the Pity*, which I was helping to promote for the Oscars at the request of distributor Don Rugoff. I somehow found myself in conversation with him and Alfred Lewis Levitt, the co-writer of *The Boy with Green Hair*, who had also worked on the American version of Henri Cartier-Bresson's *Le Retour*. By chance, we ended up standing on the street talking late into the night. In Minnelli's *The Bad and the Beautiful*, Roland's character is nicknamed "Gaucho." Norman Lloyd told me that was his nickname in real life too, and that he was beloved by everyone. I wasn't surprised.

Do you think miscasting can hold back a film, even when directed by a great filmmaker?

Just think of Ophüls' *Lola Montès*, which is undone by the casting of Martine Carol. Despite all the attempts to defend it, the film is a failure. I was at the first screening, and while I was extremely taken with its technical brilliance and the excellent performances by Peter Ustinov and Oskar Werner, I remember feeling a sense of dissatisfaction with Carol. She didn't do justice to the character, unlike Danielle Darrieux in *Madame de...*

I went back a few days later and saw it again. Contrary to what some critics later claimed, the audience wasn't confused by the film's narrative structure, they were indifferent. They didn't care about *Lola Montès*. Some have spun this into a theory, that this was in fact one of the film's virtues, but I don't believe any director ever set out for their film to be *too* slow, their protagonist *too* mad, or any of those other clichés. Ophüls cast Martine Carol because her star power helped secure funding, but if he had cast a different actress, *Lola Montès* would have been a different film — richer, more alive. And perhaps even successful.

You could raise similar questions about Renoir's *The Rules of the Game*. Apparently the original cast included Jean Gabin instead of Roland Toutain, Simone Simon in place of Nora Gregor, Michel Simon in the role that Renoir ended up playing himself, Fernand Ledoux in Gaston Modot's part, and Claude Dauphin instead of Marcel Dalio. Try projecting that alternate cast onto an imaginary screen; it's a fascinating exercise. Would the film still have failed commercially? I didn't see it in 1939, of course, but I did see it very young, in 1952, in a version that was closer to the original, though not the restored one we know today. I was 16 and unaware that it had flopped. To me, the film made a lot of sense, and it never occurred to me that it might have been difficult for a popular audience.

Poor casting can seriously harm a film. I've never liked Walsh's *Band of Angels*, which at the time we saw as a colossal failure. Walsh later admitted that he regretted not being able to make the film with Natalie Wood, who would have been around 18 then. He had wanted someone young and impressionable, whose life would be completely upended by circumstance. That said, Clark Gable didn't convince me in the film either.

Do you think the Mac-Mahon Four Aces—Lang, Losey, Preminger, Walsh—can still serve as a reference point for someone trying to understand mise en scène?

Michel Mourlet's short text on Walsh puts it very clearly: mise en scène is an exact science whose parameters remain unknown, which means even filmmakers themselves can get it wrong. There is something shared across all classical cinema. In a certain way, Renoir, Grémillon and Becker don't film all that differently from one another, just as Hanns Schwarz and Max Ophüls, or Fritz Lang and Joseph Losey, aren't as far apart as one might think. Other filmmakers, like Martin Scorsese in *Mean Streets*—his best film—have shot more exuberantly, but it's the vitality he draws out of his actors that creates a sense of authenticity. The camera isn't placed as it would be in a Lang, Walsh or Mizoguchi film, but it still grasps what needs to be grasped.

Capra, McCarey, La Cava, Cukor—all of them, really—rarely placed the camera themselves. At Columbia, the cinematographer Joseph Walker was apparently very important for Capra. He also worked on some of McCarey and La Cava's films. He positioned the camera in the simplest, most discreet way possible, and the trust that Capra, McCarey and La Cava placed in him echoes something Walsh used to say, that once the director had given the actors the right emotion and rhythm, camera placement naturally followed. The cinematographer and the camera operator would instinctively find the right lens and the right position for the shot.

Among contemporary filmmakers, Eastwood has an extraordinary instinct for where to put the camera. More recently, I discovered the Japanese-Korean director Lee Sang-il because of his 2013 remake of Eastwood's *Unforgiven*. His feel for space, air and the bitter cold of Japan's north is remarkable. His empathy for the Ainu— Japan's Inuit-like indigenous people—is palpable. It's a film that deserves urgent attention.

I also think of the 2014 Indonesian film *Siti*, directed by Eddie Cahyono, whose shot construction has a crystal-clear clarity and from its opening images evokes Preminger. The shots in which Siti, a young woman, speaks to her now-paralysed husband are wonderful. The emotional depth on her face is quietly overwhelming. It's a film that is also well worth discovering. Better known, though still underrated, is Australian director Rolf de Heer, whose *Charlie's Country* achieves great intensity in its close-ups, which, thanks to the lighting, seem to reflect the whole surrounding world.

What film best encapsulates your idea of mise en scène?

Raoul Walsh's *Objective, Burma!* The film presents an extraordinary challenge, one Walsh must have understood, at least pragmatically. The war sequences demanded absolute precision because the audience has to see exactly how a commando unit advances, how a soldier moves from one tree to the next. The constant threat behind every leaf could only be conveyed through mise en scène; there was no screenplay to rely on. If there's one film that still comes to mind today as a demonstration of what cinema is—cinema, pure and simple, and through it the world, in wartime conditions—it's that one. No other film makes you feel so intensely the physical effort, the sweat, the exhaustion, the fear. I also think of Preminger's *Whirlpool*, perhaps the clearest, most exact definition of mise en scène through editing, at once analytical and synthetic.

Curiously, I recently watched *Two Smart People*, a virtually unknown film by Jules Dassin, made before the works that made his name. And yet, quite surprisingly, it shares that same quiet professional mastery. Without disowning what we said back in the Mac-Mahon days, I now believe that beyond the Four Aces there are lesser-known filmmakers, overlooked at the time, who define cinema in a similar spirit: Urban Gad, Raymond Longford, Albert Capellani, Cecil B. DeMille, Mauritz Stiller, Hanns Schwarz, Arthur Robison, Gustav Machatý. These days I'm more excited to discover a film by one of these directors—whose work we have yet to fully explore—than to rewatch even the best of Ford or Hawks for the umpteenth time. William Wellman's *Other Men's Women*, for instance, is astonishingly bold and ahead of its time.

It would be interesting to list all the different names people have given to mise en scène. In French, we say *réalisation*; in German, it's *regi*; in Filipino, *direksyon*. In Indonesian, the term for director is *sutradara*, a beautiful word that means "birth," "bringing into the world," "bringing to light." There's something poetic in that understanding of directing, as if, very early in cinema's history, it was conceived as a kind of opening to the world, a grasping of origins. *Regi*, by contrast, feels more rigid, more authoritarian. And yet, when you glimpse the fragility of a filmmaker like Lang in the intimacy of *Liliom*—its awkwardness, its naiveté—you might say he belongs more to the *sutradara* lineage than to *regi*.

Are there elements within a film that now hold your attention more than before, moments that change the way you watch them?

I was just speaking about the "intimacy" of a Lang film. That's what really fascinates me: how certain moments, even fleeting ones, reveal the filmmaker. That's something I've always found compelling. There's a remarkable moment at the end of *Love Affair* when Charles Boyer suddenly realises that Irene Dunne has been in an accident, and that's why she didn't show up to their meeting. It lasts barely a fraction of a second, but it's the kind of moment that lets you glimpse a director's inner world. *Going My Way*— almost never mentioned by McCarey's admirers, perhaps because the characters are priests—is also a deeply intimate film.

At the end of Raoul Walsh's *Gentleman Jim*, there's a scene, one of the most unforgettable in the history of cinema, where Ward Bond steps forward to present Errol Flynn with the world boxing championship belt. The moment Bond enters, the laughter in the room freezes into sudden, overwhelming emotion. Then a single line from Alexis Smith—so quick, so lively—brings the laughter back in a flash. That fraction of a second—what we might call *volatility*—is what moves me most. Sometimes all it takes is an actor walking down the street, or a barely perceptible pan, for something infinitely intimate to occur. That's what makes such an impact in the final moments of Ida Lupino's *Never Fear*, that last shot, when Sally Forrest, playing a young dancer recovering from polio, steps out onto the street, almost timidly. She passes people who don't even notice her. Slowly, she regains her confidence in walking.

Do you experience that sense of intimacy differently with filmmakers you actually knew?

I feel it especially with Fritz Lang. After spending a lot of time with him, I later rewatched some of his films, and the tiniest, almost imperceptible details struck me in new ways. People talk about his fascination with violence, but what strikes me even more is the fear that violence provoked in him—a fear that, paradoxically, could lead in turn to even greater violence. You really get a sense of how deeply fearful a person Lang was.

These moments of intimacy aren't exclusive to Lang, nor to thrillers; they appear just as vividly in comedies and melodramas, especially with actresses like Barbara

Stanwyck, Claudette Colbert and Jean Arthur. There's a moment in *It Happened One Night* when Colbert suddenly turns to face Clark Gable, lying on his bed. Today, with how much sound has progressed — more so than image — we would probably hear the creak of the bed, the floorboards, the faint scuff of Colbert's foot. And those tiny sounds would only heighten the emotion we already feel in that moment, when we see her watching him and realise she's falling in love.

It's paradoxical — and ironic — because neither Gable nor Colbert got along, and neither believed in the film, which they were essentially forced to make. And yet Capra's heart seems to beat in perfect rhythm with that of his characters, which is what makes for rare, precious moments like these. It's what filmmakers like Hanns Schwarz, Ophüls, Litvak, Ludwig Berger and Géza von Bolváry pursued, perhaps more deliberately. They chased after spontaneity in all its hiding places.

In films made by intelligent, cultured directors, fully in command of their tools, there's sometimes a point where things shift. And in that shift, its truth is incidentally revealed. Take Preminger's *Whirlpool*. People usually focus on the hypnosis exerted by José Ferrer over Gene Tierney. But for me, the real protagonist is Richard Conte, the husband, who is faced with the decision of whether or not to believe his wife. His psychological, emotional and moral journey is worthy of an Oscar Wilde play. We know that Preminger directed Wilde's work for the stage, and that he worked with Lubitsch, who had staged Wilde before him, so even if it wasn't deliberate on Preminger's part, the focus of the film kind of shifts, subtly, onto the husband's feelings.

I noticed long ago that Richard Conte was one of those actors who really knew how to move through the space of an apartment, across a set. Watching how he crosses from one area to another, you can tell he had an acute sense of the camera and how it perceived him. There's a moment in the film when Charles Bickford reveals a detail to Conte. Conte reacts by turning away and walking off into the room. The way he moves, clearly orchestrated by Preminger, says more than any line of dialogue. It conveys both his confusion and his resolve. I don't know how conscious that moment was, for Preminger or Conte, but when Conte learns that his wife once knew the Ferrer character, and he hesitates before overcoming the implications, there's a flash of unmistakable truth.

Losey's *The Lawless* has often been read as a social drama about racism directed towards Chicanos in a small California town. The narrative follows a disillusioned liberal journalist who moves there and falls in love with a Mexican-American journalist. But very quickly — thanks to Mainwaring's script — it's the subtle emergence of their love that becomes the true subject of the film. Another Losey film where the centre of gravity shifts is *Time Without Pity*. Losey and screenwriter Ben Barzman wanted to make a statement against capital punishment. The main character is a father, played by Michael Redgrave, seeking the truth to save his son. But in fact the real main character is the murderer. The real subject of a film isn't always the one its authors intended. The true centre of gravity often expresses the filmmaker — the artist — more clearly than the surface theme ever could.

Is there another film where you see this kind of shift in subject?

Renoir's *Boudu Saved from Drowning*. People see in it whatever they want to see. Michel Simon's character is practically a non-character; he's really just there to serve as a kind of anti-bourgeois statement. But that message is rather childish. What's really interesting are all the small details — the glimpses of Parisian streets, the apartment interiors. The scene where the boat capsizes at the end and Boudu lets himself drift with the current is quite beautiful, almost anarchic in its freedom. But the most interesting character is actually Charles Granval's, the shopkeeper who takes Boudu in.

You often stress the idea of the filmmaker's sense of space, even a "cosmic" sense of space. How does that take shape on screen? And which filmmakers are best at expressing it?

Someone like Mauritz Stiller, for instance. Suddenly, the viewer is taken aback by a series of shots, sequences, spaces and actions that come at you with the force of a cannonball, something you wouldn't necessarily expect from films like *Erotikon* or his other comedies. Anthony Mann too. From his very first western, *Devil's Doorway*, you feel an extreme command over the landscape, a sense of the cosmic emerging from it. What's striking is that with cinematographers like Guy Roe, John Alton and William Daniels, Mann composes his frames obliquely. He draws out the lines in space, giving them form and meaning, whereas Stiller frames space in a more frontal, clear and direct way. There's a sort of synthesis, an osmosis of those two approaches, in Walsh's *Pursued*, with some of the most magnificent black-and-white cinematography ever, thanks to James Wong Howe. In both Walsh and Mann, light plays a central role. It allows us to feel life and the vital forces that animate it.

It's clear that filmmakers were more effective when they had a cinematographer by their side who could help bring their vision to life. Which cinematographers stand out to you?

I don't recall that we Mac-Mahonians immediately made cinematography a central tenet of our thinking, although early on we did praise James Wong Howe's work on *Pursued*, and Ernest Laszlo for Losey's *M* and Aldrich's *Kiss Me Deadly*. Among cinematographers shaped by German Expressionism, far more has been written about Eugen Schüfftan than about Curt Courant. Yet if you compare prints struck from the original negatives of *La Bête humaine*, *Le jour se lève* and *Le Quai des brumes*, there's no doubt in my mind that Courant was the greater cinematographer. One film he lit that fascinated me is Fedor Ozep's *Tarakanowa*. The light in that film is entirely white. It's absolutely unique. That whiteness opens up the space, and expands it, until it seems infinite.

Then there's Georges Benoît, the cinematographer of most of Walsh's shorts and early features in the 1910s, notably *Regeneration*. He later returned to France and shot *In the Name of the Law* and *Justin de Marseille*, perhaps Maurice Tourneur's most dynamic French films. Was it Tourneur who imposed that visual style, finding in Benoît a perfect collaborator, or was Benoît himself a shaping force? Let's not forget that he also lit some of the finest 1930s films by Sacha Guitry and Marcel Pagnol.

Nicolas Hayer deserves mention as well. Jean de Limur's *La Garçonne* contains a succession of shots more striking than those in Bresson's *Les Dames du Bois de Boulogne*. Perhaps a part of their expressive power lies in Hayer's contribution as cinematographer. And, of course, there's Henri Alekan. His rediscovery by filmmakers like Raúl Ruiz and Wim Wenders—he lit the black-and-white segments of *The State of Things* and *Wings of Desire*—has been rightly celebrated, but he did such extraordinary work much earlier. Beyond René Clément's *The Battle of the Rails* and *Beauty and the Beast* is Clément's *The Damned*, with its remarkable photography, especially those twilight shots at sea inside the submarine.

I was recently stunned by the cinematography of Emmanuel Rojas in Manuel Conde's *Genghis Khan*. A Filipino film might seem an improbably choice for portraying the founder of the Mongol Empire, but the visual power of the film is astonishing. The lighting is extraordinarily sophisticated for a Philippine production of the early 1950s, and the framing is equally accomplished. The contribution it makes to the film's impact is unmistakable. Where does Conde's work begin and where does Rojas' end? The question is worth asking.

At the Locarno Festival, I initiated a small retrospective focused on the work of Mexican cinematographer Alex Phillips, who is less celebrated than Gabriel Figueroa, but in my view served the rhythm and energy of a film more directly, rather than simply crafting beautiful images. As Brecht once said of Caspar Neher, Phillips had a real sense for "the anatomy of action." This quality is especially evident in certain films by Roberto Gavaldón, where it translates into a remarkable grasp of the spatial field in which action unfolds, of how bodies and objects move within that space, and of how actors are blocked and choreographed.

In the same spirit of filmmaking as a team effort, it's worth highlighting the contribution of Gunther Gerzso, the painter who worked on various Mexican films, often helping to select outdoor locations that were as expressive as they were realistic, or designing interiors that conveyed the same breath of life—spaces that seemed to pulsate with energy capable of melting the film itself, sometimes even beyond the director's conscious ambition. Gerzso also co-wrote a screenplay that was quite solid, and I still hold out hope that one day we'll see a beautiful printed collection of his paintings.

To what extent have great cinematographers shaped certain films?

It's a crucial question. *The Night of the Hunter* may be the ultimate example, thanks to Stanley Cortez's cinematography. Without taking anything away from director Charles Laughton, who unquestionably brought a great deal to the film, I still wonder whether he could have expressed himself visually with such power without Cortez, who modestly described himself as a technical craftsman.

What *is* direction, really? It's the director's vision, their relationship with the actors, their grasp of the dramatic arc. But where do you put the camera? And what lens do you use? And at what distance do you place it from the performers? From what angle? When do you start and end the shot? And what lighting do you use? Directors like Lang understood and controlled all of these elements, but was Laughton focused more on the drama and his actors than on how to make it exist visually? Cortez was also credited on Welles' *The Magnificent Ambersons*, whose cinematography, to my mind, surpasses even *Citizen Kane*, and yet Cortez—whom I knew personally—was disliked by Welles and Lang. Is that why he never talked about *Ambersons* or Lang's *Secret Beyond the Door*, and always cited *The Night of the Hunter* as his favorite film? Had he sensed their unease or resistance toward him? Yet the photography in both of those films is sublime.

Since the advent of digital, I have admired the look of certain films more than others, but to this day I've never seen anything that matches the splendour of films of the analogue past. There are fewer focal planes, less perspective, less vibration in the light, the air, the skin. That said, whether revolutionary or not, digital hasn't changed the way Clint Eastwood positions his camera. He's lost none of his narrative fluidity.

And yet, very few cinematographers have successfully transitioned to directing.

That's true. Among the truly great directors, Josef von Sternberg is the notable exception. Some cinematographers did make films we've never seen—Bert Glennon, for example. But how many of them actually got the chance to direct? The same applies, more or less, to screenwriters. Many have gone on to direct, but how many became truly great directors? Richard Brooks made some very good films, but he wasn't a great filmmaker. He wasn't Anthony Mann or Jacques Tourneur.

You mentioned the importance of Miles Davis' music in Elevator to the Gallows. *Are you sensitive to film scores in general?*

Yes, though unfortunately too often in a negative way. I can't stand those pseudo-symphonic scores that distract from the film rather than serve it. So many films are afflicted by this kind of music; I couldn't possibly list them all. But of course, sometimes the music is an essential narrative element. In *Time Without Pity*, Tristram Cary's powerful score meshes with the actors' performances and becomes one with the film. The same goes with Gerhard Becker's music in *The Indian Tomb*, which, in my opinion, blends more seamlessly with the other elements than Michel Michelet's score for *The Tiger of Eschnapur*, the first part of the diptych. And if we're talking about a true symbiosis between direction and music, it's impossible not to mention how Ennio Morricone served Sergio Leone's films. In *Once Upon a Time in the West*, each character, even the relatively minor ones, is accompanied by their own musical motif. The way the main theme bursts forth for the first time—when the boy's face is seen in close-up as he discovers his murdered family—shows how the music is not just an accompaniment but almost a form of writing. It becomes one of the film's driving forces. For me, it's in that film that their collaboration reached its most perfect form.

Film restorations have allowed us to discover certain films for the first time, or to see others more clearly.

I remember seeing the original version of *The Big Sleep* in London, which at the time was virtually unknown. I was struck by how much better it was, more personal, than the version we had known for years. There is less of Lauren Bacall's character in it; she is pushed more to the forefront in the original, more glamorous cut. And a deleted scene helps clarify the moral perspective of Bogart's Marlowe. The way Hawks aligns himself with that stance makes the scene with Elisha Cook Jr. far more moving than I remembered. That scene encapsulates Hawks' ethical worldview.

Conversely, have there been restorations that you feel were mishandled?

From the very beginning of cinema, image quality was remarkably high. In the 1920s, there were peaks—whether in black and white or in colour—that have never really been matched since. But that also carries a risk. The first time I truly felt that was in 1972, in Los Angeles, watching a so-called restored print of Stroheim's *Foolish Wives*. This much longer version had been assembled from different sources, prints of various generations., and within the same scene shots might have completely different lighting, which disrupted the visual, dramatic and emotional continuity. A print like that should be reserved for researchers, something to study at the editing table. In such cases, two restorations should really be made available: one that preserves continuity, and another that respects the visual style and colour grading, even if that means leaving some material out. The restoration of *L'Atalante* is another example. Some unused shots found among the rushes were added to the film. But was that really necessary? True, Vigo wasn't physically present in the editing room at the end, but testimonies suggest he followed the process closely, through friends like the poet and writer Claude Aveline, and that the original version was very close to what he intended. I remember watching a 16mm print at the Alliance Française in Bangkok. The print had very little contrast—it was all grey tones. But I felt those greys matched the film's atmosphere: the canals, the early mornings. By increasing contrast in a newer print, they actually worked against the intent of Boris Kaufman's cinematography, which was obviously developed in collaboration with Vigo. The same is true of the sound. At the time, mixing was nothing like what it is today. Sounds bled into each other, creating a kind of musical refrain that fit perfectly with the film's tone. Vigo could never have imagined the type of mix done in the late 1980s. The more technically refined audio of the restoration, with its distinct layering and polish, actually undercuts the film's original feel.

Are you enthusiastic about 4K film scanning, currently seen as the gold standard of restoration?

They can be remarkable, certainly. But perspective is essential. It all depends on the source material, the budget, the lab, the technician. I've seen some excellent restorations, and others that, despite the good intentions, seemed to betray the original version I remembered. Thanks to the quality of its technicians and lab equipment, L'Immagine Ritrovata at the Bologna Cinematheque is doing vital work digitising nitrate prints, often producing excellent results. But restoration that acts like a kind of detergent—scrubbing the image too clean—is, in my opinion, a mistake. When contrast is pushed too far, when every bit of "noise" or defect is scrubbed away, when the sound is rebuilt and each element separated, the result can strip a film of all its charm.

Which filmmakers, in your view, are overdue for rediscovery today?

Michael Curtiz, long dismissed and undervalued. *The Strange Love of Molly Louvain* is a film of remarkable vitality. The way it flows—driving the image forward, carrying the action—almost conceals just how masterfully, how discreetly, it is crafted. It's nearly a New Wave film. On top of that, Curtiz never lost his sense of spectacle, something many young, intellectual, self-important filmmakers never even tried to learn. Just look at the biblical scenes in *Sodom and Gomorrha*. They're magnificent, a true spectacle in the noblest sense of the word.

I recently saw a stunning film by Alfred E. Green called *Union Depot*. There's no doubt that the 1930s and '40s are full of filmmakers who were overlooked or forgotten, and whose work deserves reevaluation. William Seiter, for example, in *Three Blind Mice* and *The Affairs of Susan*, shows a remarkable grasp of invisible editing and for shooting with a neutral lens. There is a fluid progression from one gesture to the next, from one shot to another, all in motion, without the slightest sense of rupture, even though the angles change completely.

You have said you like films with a distinct voice or perspective. Who do you think has that among French filmmakers today

I would mention Olivier Assayas, whose elegance and ease I admire. He has achieved a beautiful fluidity in storytelling. He's a talented filmmaker, one of the few who still interest me, and I look forward to whatever he does next. Benoît Jacquot is another, perhaps more for *Deep in the Woods*, with its elliptical structure, or *Three Hearts*, than for *Farewell, My Queen* or *Diary of a Chambermaid*.

My old comrade Bertrand Tavernier had always made bold films. Some I prefer more than others: *The Judge and the Assassin, Death Watch, Coup de torchon, L.627* and *Captain Conan* are among my favourites. The character of Conan, for instance, has a psychological complexity that is all too rare in cinema. *The Princess of Montpensier*, I feel, suffers from casting missteps. Gaspard Ulliel and Mélanie Thierry should have been younger, given the characters' ages in Madame de Lafayette's novella. I also think Bertrand was mistaken in including a sexual relationship, which goes against the grain of the original story. The absence of consummation was, in a way, written into the DNA of the story, and including it, I think, slightly undermines the emotional integrity of the film. That said, in terms of its visual execution and narrative construction, it's a remarkable work.

What are the most recent films that gave you that same impression?

Wild Tales by the Argentinian filmmaker Damián Szifrón, which we have already mentioned, for its ferocity and humour. Compared to the typical films of today, which go out of their way not to offend anyone, it's exhilarating. Szifrón's direction adjusts itself perfectly to each segment of the film. He has total command of cinematic language and uses it with richness and precision; his direction lifts and carries the screenplay. The film was well received, but in my view not nearly celebrated enough, considering its talent, tone and quiet ambition.

Among younger Americans, I admire the work of Alexander Payne and James Gray. We spoke earlier about Roger Vailland's gift for dramatising social and economic forces through individual characters. Gray achieves something similar when he depicts worlds like the mafia, family, and the police. You sense his deep knowledge of film history, and behind the apparent classicism of his style lies a rhythm and vibration entirely his own, far from anything academic, flashy or showy. I find many of those same qualities in Alexander Payne's work, particularly in his psychological precision and deep understanding of character. It seems to me these filmmakers aren't revered as they should be, especially in their own country, where mediocrity is so often rewarded and where the studios are clogged with loud, mediocre directors.

I would also mention the five films of Korean filmmaker Lee Chang-dong, four of which I feel especially close to. They are pure expressions of a noble soul, something extraordinarily rare today. Through his humble and often rough-edged characters, there radiates such deep empathy for others—so human, so unguarded and raw—that it reaches you very profoundly. Over the years I have come across many people in this field who preach honesty and integrity in their work but behave dishonestly in life. Others puff themselves up as cinematic heroes and resisters, yet in real life are nothing more than cowardly and craven. Lee Chang-dong, who was once Minister of Culture in his country, is someone who has never betrayed his values.

In the end, your utterly unconventional path through the world of cinema was also something of a blessing, wasn't it?

I have been very lucky, yes, but also had my fair share of bad luck. And I think I could have done a better job handling both. This might sound terribly arrogant, but I believe I have an eye. I know cinema, and I suspect some people were afraid of my opinion, of what I might say about a script, a batch of rushes, a rough cut. They chose not to work with me. At times I was too indecisive and didn't have the courage to fight to convince the fools. I probably should have been more diplomatic and more cautious, less fiery or rigid in my convictions. But then again, that's the price you pay for being able to shave in the morning without too much shame.

FILMOGRAPHY
AND BIBLIOGRPHY

Director
La Passe de trois (1961) (short)
Les Genoux d'Ariane (1961) (short)
One Night Stand (aka *Alibis*, 1977)
Cinq et la peau (1982)

Assistant
La Chatte (Henri Decoin, 1958)
Pourquoi viens-tu si tard? (Henri Decoin, 1959)
Les Cousins (Claude Chabrol, 1959) (intern)
Breathless (Jean-Luc Godard, 1960) (first assistant director)
Les Petites Demoiselles (Michel Deville, 1962)
Paris Erotika (24 heures d'un Américain à Paris)
　　　(José Bénazéraf, 1963)
À cause, à cause d'une femme (Michel Deville, 1963)

Executive producer
The Piano (Jane Campion, 1992)
Through the Olive Trees (Abbas Kiarostami, 1994)
The Glass Shield (Charles Burnett, 1994)
Secrets & Lies (Mike Leigh, 1996)
A Taste of Cherry (Abbas Kiarostami, 1997)
Boesman and Lena (John Berry, 2000)
L'Anglaise et le Duc (Éric Rohmer, 2001)
Chihwaseon (Im Kwon-taek, 2002)
In the Cut (Jane Campion, 2003)

Editorial consultant

A Touch of Zen (King Hu, 1969)
The Valiant Ones (King Hu, 1975)
Jaguar (Lino Brocka, 1979)
Bayan ko (Lino Brocka, 1984)
Mansion by the Lake (Lester James Peries, 2002)
The Silent Army (Jean Van de Velde, 2008)

...and many others

Documentaries about Pierre Rissient
Pierre Rissient: Man of Cinema (Todd McCarthy, 2007)
Pierre Rissient, un passeur au cinéma (Benoît Jacquot,
    Pascal Mérigeau and Guy Seligmann, 2015)

Publications
Losey (Éditions universitaires, 1966)

Amarcord (Fellini), 19

INDEX